The Church as Idea and Fact

Zacchaeus Studies: Theology

General Editor: Monika Hellwig

The Church as Idea and Fact

by
Daniel Donovan

Michael Glazier
Wilmington, Delaware

About the Author

Daniel Donovan studied theology at Laval University in Québec, the Biblical Institute in Rome, and at the Wilhelmsuniversität in Münster, Germany. He is currently teaching Systematic Theology and the History of Modern Theology at St. Michael's College in the Toronto School of Theology.

First published in 1988 by Michael Glazier, Inc. Copyright 1988 by Michael Glazier, Inc. All rights reserved.

No part of this publication may be reproduced or transmitted in any form or by any means, electronic or mechanical, including photocopy, recording, or any information storage and retrieval system, without permission in writing from the publisher: Michael Glazier, 1935 West Fourth Street, Wilmington, Delaware, 19805.

Library of Congress Catalog Card Number: 88-81139
International Standard Book Numbers:
  Zacchaeus Studies, Theology: 0-89453-680-X
  THE CHURCH AS IDEA AND FACT: 0-89453-685-0

Cover Design by Maureen Daney
Typography by Phyllis LaVane
Printed in the United States of America.   SM

*To my colleagues and students,
past and present,
at St. Michael's College*

TABLE OF CONTENTS

Editor's Note 9

1. Jesus, The Kingdom and The Church 11
2. Vatican II—Renewing The Church 27
3. A Community Rooted In Mystery 44
4. Structuring The Community Of Faith 61
5. The Church, The Churches, and The World 78
6. The Church: An Introductory Bibliography 94

Editor's Note on Zacchaeus Studies

This series of short texts in doctrinal subjects is designed to offer introductory volumes accessible to any educated reader. Dealing with the central topics of Christian faith, the authors have set out to explain the theological interpretation of these topics in a Catholic context without assuming a professional theological training on the part of the reader.

We who have worked on the series hope that these books will serve well in college theology classes where they can be used either as a series or as individual introductory presentations leading to a deeper exploration of a particular topic. We also hope that these books will be widely used and useful in adult study circles, continuing education and RENEW programs, and will be picked up by casual browsers in bookstores. We want to serve the needs of any who are trying to understand more thoroughly the meaning of the Catholic faith and its relevance to the changing circumstances of our times.

Each author has endeavored to present the biblical foundation, the traditional development, the official church position and the contemporary theological discussion of the doctrine or topic in hand. Controversial questions are discussed within the context of the established teaching and the accepted theological interpretation.

We undertook the series in response to increasing interest among educated Catholics in issues arising in the contemporary church, doctrines that raise new questions in a contemporary setting, and teachings that now call for wider and deeper appreciation. To such people we offer these volumes, hoping that reading them may be a satisfying and heartening experience.

Monika K. Hellwig
Series Editor

1

Jesus, The Kingdom, and The Church

In the synoptic gospels the focus of the preaching and concern of Jesus is not the Church but the kingdom or reign of God. Following his baptism by John, Jesus begins his public life by proclaiming: "The time is fulfilled, and the kingdom of God is at hand; repent, and believe in the gospel" (Mk 1:15). What exactly he understood by the term "kingdom" is never spelled out.

The image of God as king or ruler was widespread in the ancient world. Israel adopted it, sometimes to reinforce its own monarchy and sometimes to call it into question. The hope for a renewed future came to be expressed in terms of a definitive exercise of God's kingship in the world. The images that were developed to express this varied, but they always suggested peace, justice and a certain fulness of life. It would be a time when creation would come into its own, when God's will would be done, when sin and evil would be overcome. For some this would happen in history and would mark a new moment in God's relationship to human beings; for others it would be brought about by a dramatic apocalyptic event that would overturn the present order and usher in a new heaven and a new earth.

Everything we know about the life and activity of Jesus reveals his conviction that with him something new and definitive was taking place. The God of creation and exodus, the God of Abraham and the prophets, was again at work. Jesus announced that fact as good news and invited people to faith and newness of life. Central to his message was the call to conversion or *metanoia*. It meant a change of mind and heart, a turning of the whole person to God and to his offer of forgiveness and mercy; it implied a willingness to live according to the divine will.

The NT Greek word for Church is *ekklesia*. It means an assembly; it suggests a coming together of people in response to a call. Used by various groups or gatherings in the Hellenistic world, the Jews of the diaspora had recourse to it to translate the Hebrew *qahal,* a favorite OT word to describe Israel as the assembly or people of God. Given the prominence the word came to have in the post-resurrection community, it is surprising to learn that it is almost entirely absent from the gospels. It occurs only twice and both times in Matthew. In the more significant of the two passages the reference is to the future. Jesus calls Peter the rock upon which he will build his Church (Mt 16:18). The uniqueness of the formulation together with the kingdom-oriented thrust of the message of Jesus have led scholars to doubt the historicity of the text. Some have suggested that it should be seen in relation to the last supper; others have discerned in it an Easter motif.

The world in which Jesus lived was a world that was filled with hopes and forebodings of an eschatological nature. The prolonged subjection of the Jewish people to foreign powers seemed to some to indicate that God would soon intervene on their behalf and bring the whole historical process to an end. Such a hope was a central element in the ethos of the monastic community at Qumran. Some of the sayings of Jesus, too, point in the same direction (Mk 9:1). A sense of the nearness of the end was clearly a dominant feature of early Christianity. The difficulties that it created among believers at Thessalonica are well known.

As much as the focus of Jesus' preaching was on the kingdom, the incipient Church had no difficulty in seeing its own development rooted in, and in some sense foreshadowed by, the whole of his public ministry. This is the great lesson of the gospels. If Paul made the death and resurrection of Jesus the center of his preaching and theology, the very existence of the gospels manifests how spontaneously early Christianity saw itself in relation to the first disciples of Jesus.

By his preaching and miracles Jesus attracted followers. Some of these accompanied him on his travels. He himself chose twelve from among them to share to some degree in his mission. Although subsequent tradition tended to identify the twelve with the apostles, the two groups are to be distinguished. The word apostle, meaning someone who is sent, is intimately tied up with the resurrection experiences and with the actual formation of the Church. The twelve, on the other hand, are at home in the historical life of Jesus and function there as a kind of parable in action. They are to be related to the widespread conviction that the definitive in-breaking of God's kingdom would be accompanied by the reconstitution of all of the twelve tribes of ancient Israel. Although Jesus himself seems to have promised them an eschatological role (Lk 22:30), the gospels portray them as sharing in his mission of preaching and healing (Mt 10:1ff; Mk 6:7ff). It is easy to see why the post-resurrection Church tended to identify them with the apostles (Rev 21:14) and why it was in particular that Luke saw them collectively as constituting the firm historical basis on which the faith of the Church would henceforth rest (Acts 1:15-26).

The modern study of the gospels has revealed just how little their authors were interested in the kind of psychological and historical detail that fascinates people today. Although they took the life and preaching of Jesus very seriously, they were the heirs of decades of tradition during which stories and sayings had been molded and formulated in relation to contemporary problems and questions. They themselves were anxious to present their accounts in ways that would reinforce the faith of their own communities. As a result it is impossible to write a biography of Jesus. It is in particular extremely difficult to reconstruct how he perceived and reacted to his approaching death. The growing opposition to his mission as well as the general political climate of the time must surely have alerted him to the possibility of a violent end. The human drama evoked by the story of Gethsemani and the account of the crucifixion underline the struggle that he had to undergo in order to integrate what was happening into his understanding of his mission. It is within the context of this dawning awareness and this struggle that the last supper has to be situated.

Meals played an important role in the public life of Jesus. By them he proclaimed his relationship to various people including social outcasts. In the latter cases the meals became a source of scandal to the self-righteous (Lk 15:1f). In all the gospels the last supper, whether presented as a passover meal or not, was a special moment indeed. In the synoptics it is the occasion for the institution of the eucharist. The mysterious words said over the bread and the wine sum up and define the life of Jesus in terms of self-giving love, a love rooted in his special relationship to the Father and marked by total fidelity to his mission, even unto death. The instruction to do this in memory of him pointed beyond his death to a time when the disciples would once again gather. The early Church saw its celebration of the eucharist as a response to the Lord's express command.

The resurrection is clearly a crucial moment in the whole process. Although it is all but impossible to reconstruct in any detail the events that separate the death of Jesus from the enthusiastic proclamation by the apostles that God had raised him to the fulness of life, it is these events that were decisive for the development of the Church. Most of the appearance narratives are clearly intended to ground and justify the mission and teaching of the apostles. In Matthew there are two appearances, the first to the women who had come to the tomb, and the second to the eleven disciples gathered on a mountain in Galilee. The latter scene could not be more solemn. It defines a great deal of what the Church is all about. "And Jesus came and said to them, 'All authority in heaven and on earth has been given to me. Go therefore and make disciples of all nations, baptizing them in the name of the Father and of the Son and of the Holy Spirit, teaching them to observe all that I have commanded you; and lo, I am with you always, to the close of the age'" (Mt 28:18-20).

Many of the details of this passage are typically Matthean. His gospel, written in the 80's, reflects a conscious turning of an at least partly Jewish Christian community to the universal mission. The charge of the risen Christ echoes and fulfills the promise implicit in the story of the magi. The history of the early Church reveals that this turn was not self-evident, nor did it take place without conflict. It is attributed here to the risen Lord because believers in general understood the mission and destiny of the Church to be profoundly dependent upon him. The text itself affirms the abiding presence of Jesus with the community of his disciples.

Luke-Acts contains a similar message, only now the single event of the resurrection is extended over a period of fifty days. The Easter appearances point forward to a coming of the Spirit which will enable the disciples to carry out their task of witnessing to all that Jesus has said and done. Pentecost marks the fulfillment of that promise and with it the beginning of the public preaching that is to call the Church into existence.

As important as Easter and Pentecost are, however, they do not constitute by themselves the definitive and final founding moment of the Church. Just as it has roots in the life of Jesus, so also it only gradually took on its full identity over a period of decades. Crucial in this process was the working out of the relation between faith in Christ and the following of the Mosaic law. The story of Peter and the conversion of Cornelius as told in Acts 10 attributes this decisive moment to an intervention of the Holy Spirit. The so-called council of Jerusalem, in its turn, shows how the community leaders ratified that decision in their own name.

What is true of this question is equally true in regard to Church leadership. Although the apostolic office was regarded as fundamental and was seen to be rooted in the resurrection, there was no single understanding of it. The first chapter of Acts identifies the apostles with the twelve and makes as a condition for membership in the group that one should have been a companion of Jesus during his ministry and a witness of his resurrection. Paul, on the other hand, emphasizes missionary activity. For him, an apostle in the strict sense is someone, like himself, who experienced the risen Lord and who received from him the mandate to preach the gospel (cf. Gal 1 & 2).

This absence of any kind of pre-established pattern was even more the case with leadership within the local communities. People responded in faith to the apostolic preaching and came together. The continued existence of such communities, especially outside of Jerusalem, required some kind of on-site leadership. Nothing in this regard, however, seems to have been laid down by Jesus or, at least in the beginning, by the apostles.

A key text for the understanding of the development of the ordained ministry is Acts 6:1-6. From the outset the Jerusalem community was a mixed one. Some of its members were Aramaic-speaking Jews from Palestine, while others came from the largely Greek-speaking diaspora. The two groups differed in religious sensitivity as well as in their general culture. Their varied backgrounds seem to have been a source of tensions. According to Acts these came to a head around the issue of financial support for the widows of the Hellenistic group. An appeal was made to the apostles to rectify the situation. They countered by saying that their own preaching responsibilities prevented them from exercising detailed oversight of such practical social and charitable considerations. They therefore invited the Hellenists to choose from among themselves "seven men of good repute, full of the Spirit and of wisdom" whom they would then "appoint to this duty."

Although subsequent generations read this text as recounting the institution of the diaconate, that was not its original meaning. In the following chapters of Acts, various of the seven are shown preaching and exercising the kind of authority that other passages associate with the presbyters or elders. Whatever the precise case was, what is illuminating about the passage for our purposes is that it suggests how the institution and structure of the early community developed: a need was perceived, and because existing structures were inadequate to meet it, something new was created.

Popular ways of talking about the founding of the Church by Jesus have sometimes given the impression that at some particular moment he more or less drew up its charter and spelled out its basic structures, endowments, and mission. Even a cursory awareness of the NT suggests that this was not at all what happened. The Church does indeed come from Jesus. It is a direct result of his whole life and ministry. He began the process by his preaching of the kingdom and by his calling of disciples. Clearly his message had social ramifications. The Sermon on the Mount suggests something of the way of life that was to be distinctive of the community of his disciples. His death and resurrection and the experience of the Spirit led believers to the conviction that in spite of apparent failure, God had indeed been with him and that he was in fact the savior. Paul more than anyone else spelled out in a rich array of imagery what it was that God had done in Christ. He called it reconciliation and redemption, salvation and expiation; he claimed that in Christ all things were being made new.

It was the preaching by Paul and the others before him of the resurrection and its significance that called together the communities that were to be known as the Church. Because the experience of the Spirit was so central to what was happening, it was believed that the major decisions being made and the developments taking place were all influenced by his inspiration. They too, therefore, were part of God's will for his Church.

Early Christianity expanded rapidly around the Mediterranean world, more or less following the path laid out for it by the Jewish diaspora. Acts portrays the process as a series of outwardly spiralling movements beginning with Jerusalem and passing through Judaea and Samaria until it embraced much of the Greco-Roman world. The book ends with Paul under house arrest in Rome, "preaching the kingdom of God and teaching about the Lord Jesus Christ quite openly and unhindered" (Acts 28:31).

The expansion was not only rapid, it was in many ways haphazard. In spite of the deep concern of Paul for maintaining unity with the Jerusalem Church, it is clear that early Christianity was marked by considerable variety. Each of the gospels, for example, comes out of and reflects a Church with its own history and structures, problems and concerns. The notable differences between the community revealed by 1 and 2 Corinthians and those presupposed by the letters to Timothy and Titus are well known. Here the situation is rendered more complex by the fact that the communities in question are separated by a forty year interval.

The Corinthian Church was marked by conflict and division. Some of this had to do with moral teaching and practice, some of it was related to doctrine. It was, moreover, a community that was known for, and prided itself on, the intensity of its religious experience. In 1 Corinthians Paul addresses in particular the issue of special gifts or charisms; he mentions speaking in tongues and interpretation, healing and the working of miracles. If any Church in the NT deserves the title charismatic, it is certainly that of Corinth.

The communities reflected in the pastoral epistles are more disciplined and organized. Timothy and Titus are portrayed as apostolic nuncios. Their task is to maintain sound doctrine and to see that worthy and responsible persons are appointed to roles of leadership within the local Churches. Much of the same preoccupation can be found in Acts, a document which was probably written at the same period.

The differences between the Corinthian Church on the one hand and the Churches reflected in Acts and the pastoral epistles on the other have led some scholars to speculate that initially some groups were purely charismatic and had no permanent institutional elements at all. This does not, however, seem to have been the case. In the earliest Pauline letter we read the following exhortation: "respect those who labour among you and are over you in the Lord and admonish you"(1 Thess 5:12). 1 Corinthians itself suggests that the first converts in a place exercised a certain leadership over the local community, a leadership that the members were called upon to respect (1 Cor 16:15f).

The truth of the matter is that in the beginning there was no one common way of organizing local communities, nor was there any agreed upon terminology for those who exercised leadership. Those whom Paul described as laboring among the believers and being over them probably did the same kind of thing as those who in Philippians and then elsewhere were called *episcopoi* or overseers. The people who performed the same functions in other communities were known as *presbyteroi* or elders (Acts 11:29f; 1 Pet 5:1-4; Jas 5:14). The terminology in the latter case was in all probability taken over from the Jewish tradition. By the time of Jesus groups of elders exercised oversight in individual synagogues.

Early Christian communities varied considerably in their rate of development as well as in their respective theological emphases and organizational structures. The variations, to some degree, were determined by the differing cultural and religious backgrounds out of which their members came. With the passage of time and with the dying out of the apostolic generation, there was an awareness that the original eschatological enthusiasm had been one-sided. It is this stage of settling in for the long historical haul that is reflected in Acts and in the pastoral epistles. The Church, its doctrine, and its leadership now come to the fore.

If from the beginning the term *ekklesia,* especially in the phrase the Church of God or of Christ, embraced all believers, it was also used of individual local communities. And so one hears in the Pauline letters of the Church at Corinth, Rome, Antioch and Thessalonica. In Ephesians and Colossians the word is used once again in a more universal way. In these letters it is the whole Church and not just the local community that is described as the body of Christ. This movement from the universal to the local and back again seems to have been a central feature of early

Christian faith and experience.

In regard to what constituted the life of the NT Church, the most obvious thing is the word. Just as Jesus' preaching of the kingdom had attracted disciples to him, so the apostolic proclamation of his death and resurrection provoked the faith response that resulted in the birth of the community. Nor did this initial act exhaust the role that the word was called to play. The message had to be understood and applied to new and changing situations.

In Acts 6:1-4 it is said that the apostles, because of their responsibilities in regard to the word, refused to involve themselves in the detailed oversight of the charitable activity of the community. Paul's understanding of his vocation was similar. He went so far on one occasion as to say that he was grateful that he had not baptized many members of the Corinthian community, "for Christ did not send me to baptize but to preach the gospel" (1 Cor 1:17). It is indicative that when Paul lists the various gifts the priority is given to apostles, prophets and teachers (1 Cor 12:28). All three groups are dedicated in different ways to the word. In the pastoral epistles, too, a considerable emphasis is placed on teaching. Those presbyters, for example, who preach and teach are worthy of particular honor (1 Tim 5:17). In a variation on the Pauline tradition, Ephesians lists the following as the gifts of the risen Lord to his Church: apostles, prophets, evangelists, pastors, and teachers (Eph 4:11).

Rooted as it was in the traditions of Israel and in the experience of the synagogue, early Christianity had a deep respect for the Jewish Bible as well as for the apostolic preaching and the teaching of Jesus. In all of these it recognized the word of God (2 Tim 3:16; Heb 4:12f). It was a word that called people to faith and conversion. It encouraged believers to live up to, and to persevere in, their baptismal commitments. If the Church was in a real sense created by the word, it existed in order to proclaim it.

From the beginning Christianity had its own distinctive rituals. Whether influenced by Jewish proselyte baptism or by the practices of Qumran and other sects, entrance into the Church was marked by immersion in water. When the people asked Peter on the first Pentecost what they were to do in response to his preaching of the good news, he told them: "Repent, and be baptized every one of you in the name of Jesus Christ for the forgiveness of your sins" (Acts 2:38).

The eucharist rapidly became a central feature of Church life. Although initially celebrated within the context of a meal, it soon became separated out and was joined to the synagogue service of biblical readings and homily. At an early date Paul emphasized its significance for the life of the Church. He called the sharing of the bread and wine a communion, a *koinonia,* a participation in the body and blood of Christ. Nor was this to be thought of in an individualistic sense. "Because there is one bread, we who are many are one body, for we all partake of the one bread" (1 Cor 10:17).

That Paul understood the implications of the eucharist for the Church in a very concrete way is evident in his judgment on those wealthy members of the Corinthian community who indulged themselves to excess during it while the poor went hungry. Such disregard for members of the body of Christ means that when they come together "it is not the Lord's Supper that [they] eat" (1 Cor 11:20). What Paul says here so forcefully and in relation to a particular situation is implied by John's account of Jesus' washing of the disciples' feet (Jn 13:1-16).

There is a well known passage in Acts that suggests the basic elements of the early Church's life. Those who joined the community, it says, "devoted themselves to the apostles' teaching and fellowship, to the breaking of bread and the prayers" (Acts 2:42). The theme of *koinonia* or fellowship has just been referred to in relation to the eucharist. It will come back again in our examination of certain NT ecclesiological formulations. For now, it is striking to see it listed along with word, prayer, and sacrament as an absolutely fundamental aspect of the life of faith. To become a Christian for the NT was to enter into a community, to become a member of a new family. Believers liked to call one another brothers and sisters. A cherished gift among leaders was hospitality. In Jerusalem, according to Acts, the sense of fellowship extended to the point where they held their goods in common (Acts 4:32-35).

Although the focus in early Christianity was on the life and teaching of Jesus and on the salvation that he had won, it was inevitable that thought should also be given to the Church itself, its nature and structure, its relation to Jews and Gentiles, its mission in the world. Sometimes these themes were dealt with explicitly as in Acts and in many of the Pauline letters. Sometimes one has to read between the lines. This is very much the case with Luke and Matthew, both of which represent communities which were confronted by changed historical situations and were struggling to resolve questions of identity and mission.

NT ecclesiology is dominated by the use of images. Some of these, like the field or vineyard, are evoked in passing. Others are more fully developed. The following brief examples are indicative of the way that the early Church reflected on itself.

1 Peter combines a number of OT themes and images in a passage of extraordinary theological import. The newly baptized are urged to draw near to Christ. "Come to him, to that living stone, rejected by men but in God's sight chosen and precious; and like living stones be yourselves built into a spiritual house, to be a holy priesthood, to offer spiritual sacrifices acceptable to God through Jesus Christ" (1 Pet 2:4f). Faith in Christ is never an isolated experience. Believers form together a spiritual temple, a house of God. Theirs is a community in which God dwells. Because they have been baptized in Christ and live by his Spirit, they are empowered to live the kind of life that constitutes authentic sacrifice, genuine religion, what Paul calls "spiritual worship" (Rom 12:1).

It would take a book to unpack all that this one text contains. The notion of a priestly people, for example, evokes the covenant tradition of Israel (Ex 19:5f). The theme of spiritual sacrifice has roots in the psalms and was widely although variously used in contemporary Judaism. It is present in Paul's teaching on the sacrificial meaning of Jesus' death and on the cultic significance of the whole life of discipleship. It has parallels with Hebrews' unique and grandiose vision of Christ the great high priest whose life of obedience, love, and fidelity represents the once and for all sacrifice by which expiation and forgiveness have been won.

What, in the present context, needs to be underlined in the passage in 1 Peter is its corporate emphasis. It is not said that believers are individually priests but that they together constitute a holy priesthood. This is reiterated a few verses later. The point is made even more strongly, however, by the addition of a second theme, that of the people of God. Here the OT background is provided by the prophet Hosea. "You are a chosen race, a royal priesthood, a holy nation, God's own people, that you may declare the wonderful deeds of him who called you out of darkness into his marvellous light. Once you were no people but now you are God's people; once you had not received mercy but now you have received mercy" (1 Pet 2:9f).

Once again the emphasis is on the community. Here as elsewhere reflection on the Church does not begin with what today is called the hierarchy but with the faithful. Everywhere in the NT, Church is understood primarily as people; it is what results when believing women and men come together and form a community of life and worship. Paul's famous image of the body of Christ makes the same point.

The idea of describing a group or social entity as a body was not original with Paul. It was something that was well known among the Stoics. It was in fact a rather obvious image to suggest the organic nature of human society with the inevitable interdependence of its members. What makes Paul's vision unique is his emphasis on Christ. The Church is the body of Christ; it is a community rooted in him and animated by his Spirit. As it is only in the Spirit that one can say "Jesus is Lord" (1 Cor 12:3), so it is by the one Spirit that Jews and Gentiles, slaves and free, are baptized into the one body (1 Cor 12:13). The rich vitality and variety that mark the life of the body are the result of the same Spirit's gifts.

As free as the workings of the Spirit are, Paul also sees the community's relationship to Christ as mediated by the sacraments. The eucharist, as already noted, is for him a corporate sharing in the body and blood of Christ. It brings people closer to one another even as it deepens their relationship to the risen Lord. Baptism, too, is both an immersion in the death and resurrection of Jesus and an entry into the community of salvation (Rom 6:3-11, 12:3-13; 1 Cor 12:1-30).

The letter to the Ephesians offers what is perhaps the most exalted view of the Church in the NT. It relates it to the divine plan of salvation, to the mystery hidden in God from all eternity and now made visible in Christ. This saving mystery is a mystery of reconcilation; it has broken down the dividing wall of hostility between Jew and Gentile and created a new humanity, a single body, a common household of faith. It is "built upon the foundation of the apostles and prophets, Christ Jesus himself being the cornerstone, in whom the whole structure is joined together and grows into a holy temple in the Lord... a dwelling place of God in the Spirit" (Eph 2:20-22).

This extraordinary vision of the mystery of Christ somehow continued in a Spirit-filled and renewed humanity is given an even wider setting in the letter to the Colossians. There the mystery of reconciliation embraces "all things, whether on earth or in heaven" (Col 1:20). Christ is "the head of the body, the church; he is the beginning, the first-born from the dead.... For in him all the fulness of God was pleased to dwell" (Col 1:18f). His reconciling power continues to be at work in the world through the community in which he dwells. Here the church takes on cosmic significance. It is related to both creation and the final consummation. An analogous message is suggested in the apocalyptic imagery of the Book of Revelation where the Church is linked with the heavenly Jerusalem, the bride of the Lamb, which will descend from on high at the close of days (Rev 21:9-14).

In such passages it is evident that for the NT the Church transcends all purely sociological and historical categories. As humanly comprehensible as so much of its life and growth is, its deepest meaning lies hidden in the divine mystery itself. To be truly understood it has to be seen in relation to the whole story of salvation, to the central content of Christian faith. It is this insight that impelled the early Church to include itself in its creeds.

As much as the NT emphasizes the whole community and the presence in it of the Spirit and his gifts, it is difficult to imagine that the Church was ever without some form of institutionalized leadership. Reference has already been made to the fundamental role played by the apostles. Among them Peter was clearly a dominant figure. One of the surprising results of modern biblical scholarship is the growing consensus among Protestant and Catholic alike about the importance of Peter to a broad cross section of NT communities. The marked emphasis on him in Matthew is well known (cf. Mt 16:17-19). Passages of comparable significance can be found in Luke (22:31f) and John (21:1ff). This last text is all the more striking because the fourth gospel as a whole manifests relatively little concern for Church office of any kind.

The NT presentation of Peter is not without its shadows. In the gospels he is often presented as rash and impetuous. It is he who urges Jesus to avoid the path of suffering and who, in turn, is rebuked as an agent of Satan. The story of his denial is spelled out in all the accounts of the passion. Nor are his negative traits restricted to the pre-Easter period. Paul finds Peter inconsistent in his attitude to Gentile believers and upbraids him in no uncertain terms (Gal 2:11-21). For all his faults and failings, however, Peter was clearly cherished as a central figure in the life of both Jesus and the early Church. Paul and Luke, for example, suggest that he was the first recipient of a resurrection appearance. In the account of Acts, his is clearly the dominant role in the initial growth and expansion of the community.

Although it is impossible to find in the NT the kind of explicit claims that are made at Vatican I about papal primacy and infallibility, the dogma does have a foundation in the rich and varied ministry that is attributed to Peter in the early Church. The developments in this regard to which the NT already bears witness point forward to the kind of developments reflected in the claims of the bishops of Rome. These claims will themselves undergo considerable change over the centuries, a process that continues even in our own day.

It has already been pointed out that local Church leadership probably existed in some form or other from the beginning. It varied from place to place and over the course of the first century underwent considerable change. The emphasis everywhere was on pastoral responsibility and on preaching and teaching. Of considerable importance, too, were works of charity, especially in regard to the needy members of the community. Surprisingly the NT is unclear about the responsibility of the presbyter/bishop for the eucharist. Given the traditional nature of Jewish society it is highly probable that those in charge did in fact preside at the community's ritual meals. This, however, is not explicitly stated.

The nature and function of the ordained ministry becomes more evident in the period of the apostolic fathers. It is with Ignatius of Antioch (c. 115), for example, that we clearly encounter for the first time what since then has remained with variations the classic structure of Catholic Christianity. Individual Churches are led by a single bishop assisted by a group of presbyters and a number of deacons. Before very long the so-called monarchical episcopate became the norm everywhere. Interestingly enough it is thought to have developed in Rome somewhat later than in

Asia Minor, perhaps toward the middle of the second century.

In subsequent periods various kinds of terminology came to be associated with the ordained ministry. Popes, bishops, and priests in particular were said to constitute the hierarchy. The language of priesthood was widely taken for granted. The notion of clergy underlined the distinction between the ordained and the laity. Such linguistic developments as well as things like mandatory celibacy were the products of time and changed conditions. To seek them in the NT would be anachronistic. That they are not to be found there, however, does not rob them of all validity. What it does do is to suggest that such things need to be examined critically in regard to both their origin and their contemporary meaning in order to see whether and to what degree they continue to serve the cause of the gospel.

Recent practice has brought back a traditional word into our vocabulary, the word "ministry." Its particularly Christian overtones are related to Saint Jerome's use of the Latin word *ministerium* to translate the NT *diakonia*. The Greek word means, quite literally, service, perhaps most commonly service at table. It was widely employed in the early Church to describe the mutual service that all Christians were called to show one another. It was also used to designate the particular functions or responsibilities involved in being an apostle or a leader of a local community.

It is a surprising fact that this basically non-religious term should have become as central as it did. The surprise, however, is dissipated once one recalls a famous saying of Jesus that in one form or another can be found six times in the gospel tradition: "He who is greatest among you shall be your servant" (Mt 23:11). All the gospels relate the phrase to the attitude of the twelve. Luke makes particularly clear that it also applies to Church leaders. He places the saying within the context of the last supper and by doing so heightens the contrast between the all-too-human attitude of the disciples and that of Jesus. In a kind of last will and testament Jesus has just confided to them the gift of the eucharist and in doing so has defined his life and death in terms of self-giving love. Without breaking stride Luke goes on to say that the twelve began to argue among themselves which of them was the greatest. Jesus responds that as common as such an attitude might be among the rulers of this world it is unacceptable among them. The Church leader is to be one who serves. As an example of what he means he points to himself. "I am among you as one who serves" (Lk 22:24-27).

Diakonia or ministry in this sense has profound christological roots. In a kind of definition of his life, Jesus once said: "the Son of Man...came not to be served but to serve, and to give his life as a ransom for many"(Mk 10:45). To accept the call to become a leader within the Christian community is to accept a responsibility of service, service to God, to Christ, to the gospel, to one's sisters and brothers. In serving in this fashion one enters into contact in a special way with the *diakonia* of Jesus. Although the word suggests nothing about the specific content of this or that concrete ministry, it does suggest the moral and religious attitude with which all Christian leadership is to be exercised. It points to the fact that all authentic ministry is meant to be a sacrament of the self-giving Jesus.

If Jesus preached the kingdom and it was the Church that came, it was because people believed that in him and especially in his death and resurrection God had intervened in a definitive way in human life. Because this intervention did not bring about the final consummation, room was opened up for a history of the Church. Rooted in the life of Jesus and nourished by the gift of the Pentecostal Spirit, it looked forward to the return of the Risen One. While attempting to walk the difficult path of discipleship, it dedicated itself to "preaching the kingdom of God and teaching about the Lord Jesus Christ" (Acts 28:31).

2

Vatican II - Renewing The Church

It is a considerable leap from the NT to Vatican II (1962-1965). Much happened in the intervening period, a great deal of which influenced both the development of the Church and the way that theologians and bishops understood its nature and mission.

A conviction of modern theology as of modern culture is that much that is human cannot be understood adequately apart from its history. This is certainly the case with nations and religions, institutions and cultures. As historical phenomena they bear the imprint of the period and the place in which they began. Their history entails an ongoing interaction between themselves and the successive contexts and situations within which they develop.

As self-evident as this truth is it is something that many North Americans tend to disregard, at least until events force them to recognize it. This happened in the US at the time of the Watergate scandals. The questions that were then raised about the presidency provoked a flurry of studies and publications on its beginnings and its historical development. Something analogous took place in Canada in the case of Québec separatism. Those for whom World War II was ancient history could not even begin to grasp what French Canadian nationalism was all about.

What applies to so much else also applies to the Church. It too was born at a particular moment and is now rich with nearly two thousands years of corporate experience. Because it has existed so long and has entered into and become a part of so many different nations and cultures, most of its attitudes, theologies, institutions, and practices only really make sense in terms of their history. The reason why the changes initiated by Vatican II came as a shock to

As Luth do the same the gap narrows.

so many people was that so little was known of the history that lay behind them. The liturgy is a good example. Changes in regard to the eucharist represent not so much innovations as the rediscovery of earlier practices. The current debate about forms of the sacrament of reconciliation is incomprehensible without an awareness that the medieval and post-Tridentine practice of private, auricular confession was unknown in the Church of antiquity.

The neo-scholastic theology that grew up in the mid-nineteenth century and that in spite of various challenges largely held sway in the Roman Catholic community until Vatican II tended to be ahistorical in its approach. The emphasis was on the eternal and the unchanging. The goal was to develop and refine definitions of the various mysteries of faith, definitions that could be understood and applied universally, definitions that would transcend the fluctuations of time and the relativity of culture.

The model to which this kind of theology had recourse in its reflection on the Church was that of the perfect society. The Church, in a famous formulation, could in its concreteness and visibility be compared with the Republic of Venice. It had its structures and authorities, its doctrines and laws, its sacraments and liturgical forms. It had, in short, everything that as a religious institution it required in order to fulfill its mission. Much of this was perceived as having been instituted by Christ himself. A few judicial references to the NT seemed to justify everything from papal claims to doctrines like those of the Trinity and transubstantiation.

This approach has proven to be totally inadequate to what a century of scholarship has shown to be the case in regard to both the beginnings and the development of the Church. As a thoroughly historical reality, one would need to study its entire history in order to have a real appreciation of it and of its changing, deepening self-understanding. A simple example can stand for many. Religious life in all its forms—contemplative and active, male and female, lay and ordained—is central to the distinctively Catholic experience of Christianity. At different times Benedictines, Franciscans, Dominicans, Jesuits, and many others appeared and in a variety of ways embodied aspects of the gospel vision. They became instruments for channeling religious fervor and for molding and giving form to the Church's life and mission. No serious reflection on the nature of Catholicism or on its future can afford to disregard such an extraordinary phenomenon.

It is obvious that in a book of this length very little can be said in detail about the history of the Church. Some things, however, are absolutely essential, and these will be evoked in relation to specific issues or in a general attempt to situate Vatican II and its ecclesiology within the context of the Catholic tradition.

John XXIII's announcement on January 25, 1959 of his intention to convene an ecumenical council caught almost everyone by surprise. In hindsight it is clear that the idea was not simply the product of a sudden inspiration. In 1948 Pius XII considered the possibility of holding a council and set up five commissions and consulted sixty-five bishops around the world about it. John himself was thinking of something like a council almost from the moment of his election. Cardinals Ruffini and Ottaviani have both claimed that they mentioned a council to Cardinal Roncalli during the conclave at which he was elected.

In his initial statement John XXIII was not entirely clear about what he hoped the council would achieve. He spoke of the need for deepening the bond of unity and of fostering greater spiritual vitality. He referred to periods of renewal in the life of the Church. A rather vague reference to non-Catholic Christians and a misunderstanding on the part of the popular media of the word ecumenical raised expectations that the council would address directly the issue of Christian unity.

The immediate preparations for the council were not promising. The large number of schemata or draft documents that were in readiness when the bishops met in Rome in the fall of 1962 did not offer the kind of coherent vision that could give the council a sense of identity or unity of purpose. It was for this reason and for their backward-looking theology that they were largely rejected. The majority of the bishops embraced what might be called the pope's spirit in regard to what was to take place. By this time he was speaking of the need for *aggiornamento,* a bringing up to date, a reformulating of traditional truths and structures in such a way as to bring them more directly into contact with the contemporary world. In an important speech inaugurating the council Pope John drew a distinction between "the substance of the doctrine of the faith" and "the way in which it is presented."

This distinction, he felt, was particularly significant for a council whose major preoccupation was to be what he called "pastoral."

Earlier councils, on the whole, had met at times of great debate and division. In such cases the task was to resolve the debate and to bring clarity of a doctrinal nature. This usually entailed a dogmatic definition. This was not, the pope said, what either the Church or the contemporary world needed. The reference here to the larger secular context is not gratuitous. The opening of the council coincided with the Cuban missile crisis and with Pope John's efforts to mediate between Khrushchev and President Kennedy.

Some of the larger concerns that motivated John XXIII come out in the following two quotations. On the eve of announcing the convoking of the council he said to his secretary: "The world is starving for peace. If the Church responds to its Founder and rediscovers its authentic identity, the world will gain. I have never had any doubts against faith. But one thing causes me consternation. Christ has been there on the cross with his arms out-stretched for two thousand years. Where have we got in preaching the good news? How can we present his authentic doctrine to our contemporaries?" (P. Hebblethwaite, *John XXIII, Pope of the Council,* London, 1984, p. 319)

On May 12, 1963, just ten days before he died, Pope John confided to two of his collaborators what amounts to a succinct statement of much of what was distinctive about his life and about the council that he convened and inspired. "Today more than ever, certainly more than in previous centuries, we are called to serve man as such, and not merely Catholics; to defend above all and everywhere the rights of the human person, and not merely those of the Catholic Church. Today's world, the needs made plain in the last fifty years, and a deeper understanding of doctrine have brought us to a new situation.... It is not that the Gospel has changed; it is that we have begun to understand it better." (Hebblethwaite, *John XXIII,* pp. 498f)

Another concern of Pope John that was taken up by the bishops was ecumenism. As part of the preparation for the council the pope created the secretariat for Christian unity and entrusted it to the German Jesuit biblical scholar Cardinal Bea. It was he who oversaw the carrying out of the historic decision to invite representatives of other Christian Churches and denominations to attend the council as observers. Bea was also given the delicate responsibility of developing a statement on the relation of the Church to the Jews and to Judaism.

If to John XXIII belongs the honor of convening the council and of determining to a considerable degree its spirit, it was, fittingly enough, the bishops themselves who finally formulated its agenda. A number of figures stand out in this regard, especially Cardinal Suenens of Malines, Belgium and Cardinal Montini of Milan. They, perhaps more than any other individuals, were responsible for giving the council its basic theme, the Church. Suenens suggested that the issues to be treated could be put under two headings, the Church *ad intra,* the Church in regard to its own inner life, and the Church *ad extra,* the Church in relation to all that is outside of it. Montini went further and in a letter of October 18, 1962 outlined a series of themes remarkably similar to those which the council eventually did address.

The future Paul VI agreed with Suenens that the focus should be on the Church. He saw Vatican II as completing in this way what had been begun at Vatican I, particularly in regard to the role of the bishops. He insisted, however, that the approach should be less juridical and more theological. It should focus on the religious dimensions of the Church and show how it is rooted in the mystery of the Trinity. He saw one session dealing with the inner life of the Church and another with its mission. He thought that a third session could treat of the Church's relations to other groups, to other Christians first of all, but also to the contemporary world. In this context he mentioned explicitly both the worlds of culture, art, and work and the great issues associated with the causes of justice and peace. It is not difficult to recognize the profound influence that Montini's views had on subsequent proceedings.

Vatican II was and remains without any doubt *the* council for ecclesiology. The first ecumenical councils, those of Nicaea (325), Constantinople (381), Ephesus (431), and Chalcedon (451), hammered out in the midst of great conflict fundamental formulations of faith in regard to the Trinity and the mystery of Christ. The sixteenth century council of Trent, on the other hand, was convened in order to define and coordinate a theoretical and practical response to the challenges of the Protestant Reformation. Vatican I (1869-70), meeting just as papal secular power was being undermined by the movement for Italian unification known as the *Risorgimento,* was prevented by political developments from completing its work. It issued only two documents, one on the notion of revelation and of Christian truth, and the other on the primacy and infallibility of the pope.

Part of the novelty of Vatican II was that it was meeting in a period of relative calm. Its task was not to resolve disputes, define doctrine, or hurl anathemas. It was, rather, to conduct a review of all aspects of the Church's life and to make recommendations about how that life could be renewed from its roots and how it could be adapted to the contemporary situation. The goal was to make the Church a more effective instrument of God's saving love and in the process to further the movement for Christian unity.

The council met in formal assembly each fall between 1962 and 1965. It produced sixteen documents of varying length and significance. These can be brought together in a variety of ways; the following suggests how they can be seen in relation to the theme of the Church.

From this perspective, the most fundamental document and one that is in a class by itself is the Dogmatic Constitution on the Church known by the first two words of its Latin text as *Lumen gentium,* the light of the nations. A series of nine other documents can be grouped together as dealing with various aspects of the inner life of the Church. These focus respectively on revelation and the Scriptures, liturgy, bishops, presbyters (a separate document deals with priestly formation), religious life, the apostolate of the laity, the Catholic Churches of the East, and Christian education. Another group deals with those who are outside of the Church. Included here are the documents on ecumenism, non-Christian religions, the missions, the Church in the contemporary world, religious liberty, and the means of communication. To many of these we will return in more detail in later chapters. The point of this preliminary overview is to suggest both the breadth of issues addressed and their fundamental unity in the basic theme of the Church.

A simple way of summarizing what Vatican II achieved and what it continues to represent is to say that it offers a vision and a program of Church renewal. It called for a renewal of its inner life, a renewal from the roots and in depth, a renewal that would be sensitive to contemporary forms and needs. The emphasis was consistently on the Church as a community of believers. What was uppermost everywhere, whether in relation to the liturgy or the apostolate, was a concern for the full and active participation of everyone. If this renewal was to be effective, however, it had to touch, and be supported by, bishops, priests and religious as well as the laity.

This inner renewal was thought of as inseparable from a radically new approach to other Christian Churches. At Vatican II the Catholic community committed itself to ecumenism and saw its own efforts at *aggiornamento* as a necessary prelude to inter-Christian reconciliation.

There was a dawning awareness at the council that the Christian world can no longer live in isolation. It is part of a much larger and in some cases more ancient religious phenomenon. For the first time, and in what will certainly prove to be an historic gesture, the Church turned at Vatican II in a positive way to the great religious traditions of humankind. The call was for dialogue and mutual respect. Given the history of Christian anti-semitism and the tragedy of the mass murder of European Jews during World War II, what it had to say on Judaism was fraught with the most controversy and the deepest emotion. Here, too, something new was begun that could not but have a marked effect.

Finally, and in this the council was faithful to the concerns of John XXIII, the whole Church was urged to adopt a new and positive attitude in regard to the contemporary world. The bishops committed themselves and the faithful to an active and collaborative involvement in struggles for justice and peace. The council offered in outline a renewed vision of Christian humanism, a vision it was hoped would inspire commitment and action.

If the intention of the bishops at Vatican II was to renew the Church in all its aspects and in all its relations, they did not intend in any sense to found a new Church. It is clear that they developed their vision with a conscious awareness of the almost two thousand year tradition that had preceded them. What they did was to remember things that had been forgotten, to shift emphases, to turn directly to the Scriptures and especially to the gospels for inspiration. To understand and to be able to judge their achievement, one has to see it within the larger historical context. Only then can the new emphases be appreciated and the underlying continuity discerned.

There are different ways in which one might attempt to relate Vatican II to the history of the Church. The present text will evoke briefly two of these. The first was suggested by Cardinal Suenens shortly after the close of the council. He said that Vatican II "marked the end of several epochs." "It brought to a close the Constantinian era, the era of 'Christendom' in the medieval sense, the era of the Counter-Reformation and the era of Vatican I" (L. -J. Suenens, "Introduction" in *Theology of Renewal,* vol II, ed. by L. K. Shook, Montreal, 1968, p. 7).

The Emperor Constantine (died 337) marked a turning point in Church history. Before him the Christian community had no legal status within the Roman world. It was a minority group profoundly at odds with elements of the dominant and state supported pagan culture. The threat to which its lack of a legal position exposed it resulted periodically in forms of persecution that occasionally took on the character of a pogrom. Before the fourth century, being a Christian was very much a voluntary act.

The acceptance of Christianity as a legal religion began a process that before very long saw it become the official religion of the empire. Far from being at odds with the ruling authorities, it came in various ways to be supported and furthered by them. Almost immediately large and impressive Churches were built, and the social and political position of bishops was enhanced. It was this new situation that developed into the pattern of Christianity that is known as Christendom. In the West popes and bishops came to exercise considerable influence in many aspects of civil as well as religious life. In the feudal period bishops fitted into the dominant structures and in some cases became the pawns of powerful kings and emperors. Following the Gregorian reform in the late eleventh century the medieval papacy became an increasingly powerful force in both Church and society. Its secular power was enhanced by the papal states, great tracts of land in central Italy which the medieval period on the whole believed had come into papal possession through what was known as the Donation of Constantine.

As important as the mutual reinforcement of state and Church was, the symbiosis of faith and culture that was so much a part of medieval society was perhaps even more striking. Western culture throughout the period was markedly Christian. Faith and reason, religion and culture were so intertwined as at times to be hardly distinguishable. It was this amalgam of Europe and Christianity that the great missionary outreach of the sixteenth and subsequent centuries was to spread around the world. The institutions as well as the theology and the religious art of the period were the product not just of the gospel but of the gospel as it had entered into and become an essential component of Western civilization.

In saying that Vatican II marked the end of the Constantinian era as well as the era of Christendom, Cardinal Suenens was underlining two things in particular. In the first place the council solemnly and explicitly accepted the de facto modern development of the separation of Church and state. In the document on religious liberty the Catholic Church for the first time clearly committed itself to defend the rights of everyone to religious freedom including the right to public and corporate expression of religious convictions. In many parts of the world, especially in North America, this had been taken for granted for some time. Elsewhere some Catholics continued to nourish a very different vision. If, for such people, religious liberty is to be insisted on when Catholics are in a minority, when they are in a majority position concern should not be for the rights of conscience but for the rights of truth. The rejection of this approach had immediate and practical implications in Spain, Portugal, and parts of Latin America. The new position made it possible for members of other religious traditions to take seriously what the council was saying about dialogue. It also provided a consistent theoretical underpinning for appeals for freedom of religion in those parts of the world where the Church found itself under repressive and atheistic regimes.

The reference to the Constantinian era and to medieval Christendom cannot help but evoke the issue of religion and culture. Traditional Western civilization has been largely Christian. In those countries where Catholicism has been the dominant religion, the culture has had a Catholic flavor. Ever since the Enlightenment, and in particular since the great revolutionary period at the end of the eighteenth century, the uniformity and the religious character of this culture has been breaking down. Contemporary Western society, whether in its European or its North American form, is the product of a complex history extending back to the medieval and ancient worlds, but profoundly modified by modern developments in science and technology as well as in the forms of political life. Many of these modern developments were achieved in a conscious struggle against traditional forms of religion. This has resulted in a more or less secularized public environment, one that is marked by a pluralism of values with a particular emphasis on the rational qualities of science and its technological offshoots.

To accept the end of Christendom in this context is to accept that the great medieval synthesis of religion and culture as well as its various and mitigated modern successors are no longer a possibility nor even an ideal. It suggests the inevitability of pluralism and of the need for the Church to develop new strategies for being present in such a society. What all this means in the concrete has been felt in an intense way over the last twenty-five years or more in the province of Québec. Here was a part of Canada that was both French and Catholic. Until relatively recently it was predominantly rural. Although the Church was in no sense established, almost all aspects of the province's education, health, and social services were provided by religious orders and congregations. The interrelation of religion, language, and culture was so intense as to make it difficult for some to be French Canadian and not to be Catholic. Now, all that has changed.

The history of the Québec Church since the council has been the history of a Church undergoing profound cultural dislocation. The old synthesis seemed to collapse almost overnight. The number of priests and religious declined dramatically. Their social and cultural responsibilities were largely taken over by the state. Large numbers of people ceased to practice their religion in any public way. The dominant culture of Québec became increasingly marked by the technological and consumer values of the rest of North America. Church leaders, showing a remarkable openness to, and appreciation of, what was taking place, have courageously accepted the task of developing new ways for the Church to be present in the changed cultural situation.

Although the story of Québec Catholicism is in many ways unique, the experience of many English-speaking Catholics has had affinities with it. Their backgrounds have been in many cases minority ones. The recent entry of large numbers of Catholics in North America into the middle class and into mainstream culture has frequently been accompanied on a personal level by a sense of cultural dislocation analogous to that experienced by Catholic French Canadians.

What is implied by Suenens' reference to the period of the Counter-Reformation is perhaps more immediately obvious to North American Catholics. The Reformation was a traumatic experience for the Catholic Church. The unity of the Western Church and of Western society was broken. Some of the particular positions that the reformers embraced were perceived as fatal for both Christian truth and Christian life. Although the council of Trent was a major factor in the development of what might be called the Catholic Reformation, the doctrines and practices that it emphasized clearly bore an anti-Protestant emphasis. If Luther wanted to stress the Scriptures and preaching, Catholicism would be known as the Church of the sacraments. If the new Protestant Churches ordained married men then the Catholic tradition would reaffirm and do everything possible to foster the celibacy of its clergy. What all this and more led to was not only a Catholic renewal, but a renewal that underlined precisely those aspects of the tradition that the Protestants had denied. This inevitably resulted in a somewhat one-sided and impoverished vision of Catholicism, one in which the Church tended to define itself too exclusively over against others. At the worst this produced a sectarian mentality devoid of all generosity in appreciating traditions other than its own.

The importance of ecumenism at Vatican II was considerable. It is something to which we will return in chapter 5. Already, however, it needs to be pointed out that the impact of an ecumenical sensitivity at the council influenced far more that just the way the bishops viewed other Christian Churches and communities. It had a profound influence on the way they regarded their own tradition. Many issues, from the importance of Scripture to the use of the vernacular in the liturgy, which had been thought of as typically Protestant, were recognized to be part of the Catholic tradition. The overcoming of a Counter-Reformation attitude opened up for the bishops the possibility of rediscovering the real breadth of their own heritage.

Cardinal Suenens' reference to Vatican I corresponds to one of the goals that Montini had set for the council. He wanted it to focus on the episcopacy in order to complement what the earlier council had said about the papacy. The very fact of calling the council had implications in this regard. It was widely felt and explicitly taught by some theologians that once papal primacy and infallibility had been defined there was no further need for a council. It was almost as if the whole conciliar and episcopal tradition of the Church was being forgotten or at least undervalued in the light of the focus on the primatial role of the pope. The simple fact of announcing that there would be a council called to mind the conciliar principle and conciliar tradition. Once a council was seen as a possibility, it was also recognized as natural and almost self-evident. A Church as large and varied as the Roman Catholic Church could not help but benefit by involving the bishops of the entire world in a process of consultation and decision-making. The experience of the council was such an encouraging one that it itself became a theme of discussion under the technical phrase "collegiality."

Collegiality is related to the word college. It was used at the council first of all with reference to the fact that in the NT, as important as Peter is, he neither exists nor acts in isolation. He is a member of the twelve, and although he is their head and spokesperson his leadership is clearly related to theirs. The history of the Church and especially the decisive role played in it by synods and councils, including ecumenical councils, is ample warrant for drawing an analogy between the collegial nature of the twelve and that of the whole episcopal body. The pope, the concept of collegiality insists, is and remains a bishop, a member of the world episcopate. It is the entire episcopate with and under the bishop of Rome that shares a responsibility for the world Church. To become a bishop is not simply to accept a position of leadership within a local diocese. It is to enter into the episcopal college, all the members of which have a corporate responsibility for the whole.

The reference to the period of Vatican I suggests something else as well. From the 1850's on the Roman Catholic Church found itself more and more defensive and judgmental about much of what was happening in Western European society. It was difficult for Church leaders to recognize the positive values represented by the French and American revolutions. The call for liberal freedoms and for democracy was often understood to be at odds with Catholicism and indeed with all religion. The problem was complicated by the so-called "laicizing" and anti-religious values of many leading European liberals. In Italy the whole situation was rendered more difficult still by the existence of the papal states. In 1864 Pius IX published an encyclical and had attached to it a list of some eighty propositions culled from his earlier writings, all of which he had repudiated as false. This was the famous Syllabus of Errors that provoked so much feeling and debate in nineteenth century Europe. Although liberal Catholics tried to nuance its meaning and reduce its significance, for many people both inside and outside the Church it added up to a resounding no on the part of the papacy to much of what was most progressive in modern thought and practice. The eightieth proposition suggests the tone of the whole document: "The Roman Pontiff can and should reconcile himself to progress, liberalism, and modern society." This, as the other seventy-nine propositions before it, was rejected as erroneous.

The psychological isolation of the papacy from modern developments was reinforced by the fact that after the taking of Rome by the troops of the *Risorgimento* in September 1870 Pius IX and his successors considered themselves prisoners of the Vatican. The situation was only normalized by the setting up of Vatican City as an independent entity by the Lateran treaty of 1929. In the immediate aftermath of what happened in 1870 and for some time thereafter Italian Catholics were forbidden to take any active part in the new state.

The problem of Catholicism and modern culture came to a head in what is known as the "modernist crisis." A series of developments, primarily in the European Church, between 1890 and 1910 represented an attempt by a number of scholars, both clerical and lay, to build a bridge between Catholicism and aspects of modern culture. The movement was at it most intense in France, but it also had representatives in England and Italy. Something separate but analogous was taking place at the same time in Germany. The individuals involved worked in a variety of areas including philosophy, Church history, and exegesis. In Italy it was more directly tied to the cultural and political situation. In spite of differences of nationality and education, of discipline and political commitment, everyone in the movement shared to some degree a common perception. They saw a dramatic gulf between the Church's life and theology and what was best in contemporary

European culture. They believed that something could and should be done to overcome it.

Inevitably mistakes were made, and positions were adopted that could not easily be shown to be compatible with the Catholic tradition. Above all many in Rome and especially in the entourage of Piux X had no appreciation for the significance of the difficult and crucial issues that were being addressed. A new syllabus of errors was issued in 1907. This was soon followed by an encyclical of Pius X entitled, *Pascendi dominici gregis.* It offered an interpretation of modernism which it then condemned as the compendium of all heresies. In order to combat it a renewed emphasis was to be given to scholastic philosophy and theology, and a greater commitment and loyalty was to be required of all the clergy. This resulted in 1910 in the imposition of the anti-modernist oath, an oath that continued to be required on a regular basis from priests and theologians right up to Vatican II.

The massive and one-sidedly negative response to the so-called "modernists" inaugurated a period of Church history known as "integralism." It was marked by rigidity, defensiveness, and suspicion on all fronts. Anything that in any way seemed to be sympathetic to modern culture was condemned as anti-Catholic and anti-religious. Although the intensity of integralism died down by the 1920's, the anti-modernist mentality remained in the ascendancy right into the 1950's. An awareness of this history underlines just how remarkable the council's openness to modern culture was. It is difficult to imagine that the same Church could have produced the Syllabus of Errors in 1864 and *Gaudium et spes,* the Pastoral Constitution on the Church in the Modern World, in 1965.

If it is a distortion to exaggerate the differences between the pre- and post-conciliar Church, it is equally mistaken not to recognize the truly historic dimensions of what was accomplished at Vatican II. Cardinal Suenens' attempt to relate it to the Constantinian era and medieval Christendom as well as to the periods introduced and symbolized by Trent and Vatican I is extremely helpful in this regard. More recently Karl Rahner has made an alternative suggestion which is equally illuminating.

According to Rahner, Vatican II marks the beginning of what he calls the third great period in the history of the Church. The first period was a relatively brief one and coincided with that moment at the beginning when Christianity was still very much a Jewish phenomenon. The second period began with the slow and often conflict-laden entry of the Church into the Greco-Roman world. The extraordinary symbiosis of Hellenism and the gospel that characterized the golden age of the patristic Church eventuated in medieval Christendom. In spite of all the changes that the post-Reformation Church had to face and in spite of all the developments it itself underwent, it remained basically European in nature. Even in the missions, the Church as a cultural reality was perceived as, and in truth largely was, an extension of Europe. At the council, according to Rahner, for the first time the Church began to become a truly world Church, a Church that would be united at its deepest level and yet authentically plural in its concrete embodiments in the various cultures around the globe.

Rahner emphasized that the council only represented a beginning in this regard. He believed, however, that a world Church was the challenge of the moment and that Vatican II in its make-up, in its desire for dialogue, and in its openness to cultural pluralism within the one faith, had taken a step in this direction. The way forward will obviously not be easy. As in the movement of the Church from its Jewish origins out into the Hellenistic world, there is no detailed road map to follow. Trial and error, conflict and debate will be as much a part of the present challenge as it was of the earlier one.

Vatican II was the council of the Church. Ecclesiology was at the heart of all its deliberations. Its concerns, we have seen, were primarily pastoral and practical although it also generated a remarkable theological vision. It called for renewal and adaptation in every aspect of the Church's inner and outer life. The attempts of Suenens and Rahner to place its efforts within the larger historical context underline just how significant and by the same token how difficult its challenge was. It is not surprising that the post-conciliar period has known conflict and that the process of implementation has encountered obstacles. An awareness of history, especially the history of earlier councils, should have alerted people to the inevitability of such problems. The very nature of the renewal called for, a renewal in spirit as well as in form, a renewal that would be both personal and institutional, was not to be achieved rapidly or without serious individual and corporate conversion.

The Extraordinary Synod of Bishops convened by John Paul II in the fall of 1985 to celebrate the twentieth anniversary of the end of Vatican II was an important moment in the history of the council's reception. The period leading up to the synod was marked by rumors and speculations of the most extreme kind. Some feared, and others hoped, that it would somehow mean the beginning of a return of the Church to its pre-conciliar stage, or at least that it would draw the line at the letter of the conciliar texts. These expectations were fed by the negative interpretation of the post-conciliar period offered by Cardinal Joseph Ratzinger in a widely reported interview which appeared in book form in 1985 under the title *The Ratzinger Report*. As the head of the Congregation for the Doctrine of the Faith the cardinal occupied a position that gave his perceptions considerable weight.

In their final report the bishops at the synod admitted that the reception of the council's teachings by the Church had not been without "deficiencies and difficulties." They spoke of "shadows in the post-conciliar period" which were "due in part to an incomplete understanding and application of the council." Realistically, however, all the troubles of the contemporary Church should not be laid at the feet of Vatican II. The world, they recalled, has changed in many ways in the last twenty years, as has the situation within the Church. These things, too, have to be considered in judging what has happened.

In spite of the negative phenomena, however, the bishops did not hesitate to call the council "a grace of God and a gift of the Spirit" and to affirm that it "is a legitimate and valid expression and interpretation of the deposit of faith" (2). The solemn conclusion of their report contains a prayer of gratitude to God "for the greatest grace of this century, that is, the Second Vatican Council" (7).

The report addresses a number of specific ecclesiological issues to which reference will be made in the following chapters. It is sufficient for the moment to recall the report's general thrust. The bishops call for a continued and renewed effort to accept and implement the council "in both its letter and its spirit" (2). The technical term that is used for this process is "reception." A Church teaching or regulation remains largely a dead letter until it is accepted and acted upon by the whole community. It was one thing to have conceived the vision of Vatican II, it is quite another to have it animate, and be embodied in, the corporate life of the Church. And so the bishops emphasized "the need for a deeper reception of the council." This, they said, "requires four successive phases: a deeper and more extensive knowledge of the council, its interior assimilation, its loving reaffirmation, and its implementation. Only interior assimilation and practical implementation can make the conciliar documents alive and life-giving" (5).

The rest of this book will try to serve this goal by relating major themes of contemporary ecclesiology to Vatican II's vision of renewal.

3

A Community Rooted In Mystery

The first chapter of Vatican II's most comprehensive ecclesiological document, *Lumen gentium,* is entitled "The Mystery of the Church." The phrase highlights the religious depths of the community of faith. As visible and as human a reality as the Church is, its ultimate identity lies hidden in the heart of Christian religious experience. It belongs to the world of faith and is only comprehensible within the context of the whole creed.

The word mystery is sometimes understood as referring to what for the moment cannot be understood but which with time will be. The number of "mysteries" in this sense that the progress of science has laid to rest is legion. Other uses of the word seem to have the function of mystifying, of deflecting critical reflection, and thus, intentionally or not, of defending the status quo. The word "mystery" in *Lumen gentium* has a different function and a deeper meaning.

In the Bible as well as in theology, mystery points to the reality of God. In the apocalyptic tradition that formed part of the context within which Christianity was born, the word was used for God's hidden plan of salvation. In Ephesians and Colossians it becomes a central category for understanding the whole Christian dispensation. It refers there to God's eternal plan to reconcile all things in Christ. "Hidden for ages and generations," it has now become manifest. Called "the mystery of Christ" (Eph 3:4), it continues to be present in the world through the community in which Christ lives (Col 1:27).

More than any other modern theologian Karl Rahner made the concept of mystery central to his theology. Influenced by the

Greek Fathers, the great mystics, and contemporary philosophy, he insisted on the incomprehensibility of God. To apply the language of mystery to God, however, is to say much more than that he cannot be understood. It affirms that he is the fulness of being and of truth, an abyss of infinite intelligibility, a darkness brighter than all light. For Rahner, God is the mysterious and incomprehensible horizon within which all life is lived out. What is distinctive of human beings is that they have a more or less conscious awareness of that horizon and relate to it in all that they do. The great claim of Christianity, according to Rahner, is that God has not been content to remain at a distance but has communicated himself to us in love. The mystery therefore is not far but near. It is at once both transcendent and immanent, beyond all that is and yet present within it. If the offer of God's own life is universal, it is made known and communicated in a special way in the person and destiny of Jesus. In him the mystery has become incarnate.

In Rahner's perspective as in that of the NT, to speak of the mystery of the Church is to underline its relation to God's plan of salvation. The inner life of the Church and its historic destiny are rooted in the whole sweep of God's relation to the world from creation to final consummation. In a special way the Church is part of and continues the mystery of Christ. This is only possible because of the presence in it of his Spirit.

The notion of mystery is intimately related to the idea of sacrament. In the early Latin versions of the NT *sacramentum* sometimes translated the Greek *mysterion* or mystery. The Fathers of the Church did not hesitate to describe Christ and the Church in sacramental terminology. Christ is the original sacrament because in him the divine mystery has become visible and accessible. The Church, on the other hand, continuing in some fashion in space and time his presence in the world, is thought of as a sign and instrument of saving and renewing grace. In this sense it is a sacrament of both Christ and his Spirit.

Grounded in the being and activity of the triune God, the Church is a mystery of union and communion. From the beginning, according to the Bible, humankind was meant to live in peace and harmony with God, among themselves, and with the world. Sin, however, disrupted the original ideal. If at the most profound level sin alienates people from God, it also sets them at odds with themselves and with one another. Modern ecological concerns have given us a new insight into just how alienated we are from the world at large. The saving act of God in Christ and the Spirit was intended to overcome the destructive power of sin and to begin the process of making the whole of creation new. It is within this perspective that the nature and mission of the Church have to be understood.

The Church is obviously an historical and sociological phenomenon. Many of its institutional and doctrinal developments reflect laws and patterns that govern comparable corporate bodies. An appreciation of such principles can facilitate an understanding of much that is going on in the Church at any given moment. As helpful as such insights are, however, they do not exhaust the reality of its inner life. At its deepest level the Church remains a mystery of faith.

The theme of mystery is a central one in the report of the 1985 Extraordinary Synod of Bishops. Looking back over the previous twenty years it said that a tendency to focus exclusively on institutional questions had sometimes resulted in blindness and insensitivity to the specifically religious dimension of Church life. This tendency was all the more unfortunate because of the growing secularism of the Western world. The bishops, therefore, called for a renewal of the sense of the sacred and for a deepened awareness of how profoundly the Church is related to the whole mystery of Christ.

If Vatican II anchors its ecclesiology in the notion of mystery, it tries to flesh it out by applying to the Church a series of images all of which are taken from the biblical tradition. The particular image that dominates conciliar thinking is clearly that of the people of God. It is the title of *Lumen gentium*'s second chapter.

Neo-scholastic ecclesiology emphasized the institutional element. Continuing a tradition that had been dominant since the sixteenth century, it developed its understanding of the Church around the concept of the perfect society. Nineteenth century romanticism, on the other hand, brought a sense of the historical and the organic. In theology this translated into a renewed awareness of the theme of the body of Christ and its Spirit-inspired life. In spite of opposition, this approach gradually won acceptance until in 1943 Pius XII endorsed it in his encyclical *Mystici corporis*. Throughout this period the emphasis on the mystical body functioned as a corrective to the institutional and juridical preoccupations of the neo-scholastic tradition. It stressed the Church's continuing dependence on the risen Christ and drew attention to the hidden and life-giving presence of the Spirit within it. An exclusive focusing on the image of the body of Christ, however, led to its own difficulties. The human reality of the Church tended to be lost from view. It was not easy, for example, to call the Church the body of Christ and to think of it as sinful. Nor was it immediately evident why it might need reform and renewal.

The image of the people of God was so dominant at Vatican II because it brought out those particular aspects of the life of the Church that the bishops believed had to be emphasized at that moment. It was of course a biblical concept, and that in itself was important. Pope John had wanted the council to be pastoral and biblical rather than abstract and juridical. He wanted to bring the human person back into the center of the Church's consciousness. From this point of view the people of God image could hardly have been more apt.

There is a sense in which the whole Bible is the story of a people. Although that story is pushed back into the mists of pre-history with the accounts of creation and sin, the flood and Babel, it really begins with the call of those whose names stand at the origin of Israel's identity, Abraham and Sarah, Isaac and Rebekah, Jacob and Rachel. It is with Moses and the exodus that the theme of peoplehood comes to the fore. The Lord leads the Israelites out of slavery in Egypt and makes a covenant with them at Sinai. He will be their God and they will be his people. It is a formula that returns repeatedly in the course of biblical history. It functions sometimes as a reminder and a challenge and at other times as a promise and a consolation. Israel's hopes, even for the end times, always maintained a strong community dimension. In Jeremiah's prediction of a new covenant, God recalls the exodus and Sinai and announces: "Behold, the days are coming, says the Lord, when I will make a new covenant with the house of Israel and with the house of Judah.... I will put my law within them, and I will write it upon their hearts; and I will be their God, and they shall be my people" (Jer 31:31-33).

By emphasizing the image of the people of God, Vatican II reaffirmed the Church's biblical roots and brought back to

Catholic ecclesiology fundamental categories like those of choice and election, covenant and promise. If the image of the body of Christ emphasizes the newness that is ours through Christ, the language of the people of God underlines our relation to the whole history of God's involvement with humankind. To speak of "people" is much less precise than to speak of an institution. There are, for example, many ways in which one can belong to a people. In a very real sense everyone who has ever lived is a member of God's people.

As most images, this one too has negative as well as positive implications. If it is a good thing for Catholics to rediscover their relationship to the children of Abraham and to the people of the covenant, it would be a tragic misfortune if in doing so they were to think that God's graciousness was withdrawn from the Jews and somehow transferred to the "new" people of God. The fact that this was often believed in the past resulted in a totally negative view of post-biblical Judaism. Christians disregarded or did not know how to deal with Paul's profound reflection on the mystery of Israel. But that is no longer the case. Today we affirm with him that to the Jews belong "the sonship, the glory, the covenants, the giving of the law, the worship, and the promises" (Rom 9:4f). We believe that they remain God's people and, if we have no simple formulation for relating their covenant to ours, we none the less proclaim its continuing validity. Paul enunciated the basic principle here: "the gifts and the call of God are irrevocable" (Rom 11:29).

An area of life where biblical experience and modern sensitivity rejoin one another is in the importance given by both to history. A so-called classical approach to culture attempted to establish a single pattern that would be forever normative. In our own day the pursuit of such an ideal has given way to an awareness of historical and cultural relativity. As individuals and as communities we are beings in time. Born at a particular moment we are molded and formed by specific cultures. If there are transhistorical and transcultural values to which we are open, even they are embedded in forms and institutions that are historically conditioned.

Although the biblical experience of history was not expressed in the categories that are used today, it was nonetheless real. It was in fact at the heart of Israel's relationship to God. For the

Bible, God is not only the creator, he is also the Lord of history. He calls Abraham and sends him on a journey; he manifests himself to Moses as the one who is with the people on their pilgrimage. The prophetic vocation presupposes a continuing presence of God to the life of humankind. The divine promises influence history and beyond every disaster open the future in new and surprising ways.

The image of the people of God read against this background suggests possibilities for understanding the Church's historical nature. Already in Hebrews the Church is portrayed as a pilgrim people still on the march, not yet at its final resting place. Its present life can be profitably compared to Israel's desert experience (Heb 4:1-11).

Given the considerable difficulty that the leaders of the Church had in dealing with the application of modern historical scholarship to both the Bible and Church history, it was essential that the council find a way of thinking about the Church that would facilitate historical sensitivity. The new moment in God's dealing with humankind in Christ seemed initially to be the prelude to the end of time. When that turned out not to be the case, the Church began its own historical pilgrimage, some of the key moments of which have already been evoked. It is a pilgrimage that has been as eventful, as challenging, and as full of grace as that of Israel. In the course of it the Church has changed and grown; it has forgotten some things and learned others. It has experienced at all levels of its life what it means to live in time.

As a pilgrim people the Church is repeatedly confronted with new challenges and new possibilities. The choices that these entail can be more or less dramatic. To deal with them the Church has to have a certain flexibility and openness. It has to know, as much as one can, what in its life and teaching is really essential and what, because it is historically conditioned, can and should be abandoned when the situation calls for it. It is clear that such decisions cannot be made beforehand, nor are they simply to be deduced from general principles. Here practical wisdom and discernment and the inspiration of the Spirit are essential.

The story of the Bible is a story of sin as well as of grace, a story of lust and greed, jealousy and hate as much as of their opposites. The history of the Church, too, is marked by all manner of moral and spiritual failings. The eucharistic liturgy begins with an invitation to those present to recall their sins and to beg for God's mercy. As much as we are called to be a sacrament of Christ, we are all acutely aware of our sins and inadequacies. Such an awareness has always been a part of the life of the Christian community. In the past, however, people hesitated to attribute sinfulness to the Church as such. It was thought of as holy, even if its members were sinners. To think of the Church as people, however, makes it easier to think of it as sinful. If we are the Church and if we are sinners, then it seems a fairly simple thing to conclude that the Church itself is sinful.

The tension between sin and holiness is endemic to all religious life. In the perspective of the Bible, God is the Holy One *par excellence*. Made in his image and likeness human beings are called to holiness of life. For Israel this involved cultic purity but even more importantly the following of God's will as expressed in the Mosaic Torah. In some of the psalms it took on a profoundly personal, almost mystical tone.

Holiness in early Christianity was associated with the Spirit. Through faith and baptism people are brought into contact with the redeeming and sanctifying power of Christ's death and resurrection. That power is made operative in them through the one whom Paul calls "the Spirit of holiness" (Rom 1:3). The perfection of life to which believers are called entails both moral and religious qualities. Most profoundly it is tied up with the idea of grace. People are holy to the extent that they share in the life of God. What this means concretely is suggested by the life and destiny of Jesus and by the moral ideal contained in the Sermon on the Mount.

If God is holy, so also are Christ and his Spirit. God's saving act in Christ is meant to call forth and nourish in people a genuine holiness of life. The Church, ideally, is to be a community of holiness, a community of saints. The means that Christ has given it to attain this goal share in his holiness. This is true of the Scriptures and of the sacraments; it is true in a special way of the eucharist. It is also true of the mysterious workings of the Spirit in all aspects of the Church's life, from the guidance he gives its leaders, to the many and varied charisms that he awakens among its members. When we turn, however, from Christ and his Spirit to our own humanity, we have to recognize with Paul that "we have this treasure in earthen vessels" (2 Cor 4:7). It is in the lives of the saints that the real nature of the Church is revealed. In them the power of the Spirit of the risen Christ to renew human life becomes manifest.

To recognize that the Church as the people of God is a sinful community is not at all to deny or undervalue the call to holiness or the presence of the Holy Spirit and his gifts within it. It is simply another way of saying that the Church has not yet arrived at its final destination, that it is still on the way. It needs, precisely as a community, as well as in its individual members, continually to hear and respond to the challenge to repentance and conversion. Bigotry, racism, sexism, arrogance, self-righteousness, all these and more have haunted the history of the Church. They deface and deny its true nature. They cry out to be left behind in a more authentic following of the pattern of Christ.

If the people of God is the dominant image at Vatican II, it should not be opposed to the image of the body of Christ. In some way the two images are complementary. If the people of God theme relates the Church to the whole range of God's involvement with humanity, then the reference to Christ brings out what is most distinctive about it. In some sense one might say that the Church is that part of the people of God that believes explicitly in Jesus as the Christ. It lives self-consciously out of his message and under the inspiration of his Spirit. Its very special task is to continue his mission, to be the sign and instrument of the salvation that he effected on behalf of all. Much of what the council had to say about this image is based on the NT. Some of that has already been developed above. Other implications of the image will be mentioned later.

A third significant image at Vatican II and an enormously rich one in the Bible and in the history of the Church is that of the temple. The Christian community is and is called to be the temple of the Holy Spirit. The idea of the temple suggests the presence of God; it also evokes the themes of prayer and worship. To relate this image to the Spirit is to stress that the life of the Church and of all its members is only possible by the gift of the Spirit. Paul defined the Christian experience in some sense when he said that "God's love has been poured into our hearts through the Holy Spirit who has been given to us" (Rom 5:5).

Vatican II brought back to ecclesiology a sense of the importance of charism. The word comes from the Greek and means a gift. In a Christian context the implication is that it is a gift of the Spirit. The inspiration for the council's views on charisms comes from the NT and especially from Paul's classical texts on the subject. 1 Cor 12:1-31 and Rom 12:3-8 relate the idea of gifts to the concept of the Church as the body of Christ. All are members of the body and all receive gifts although these vary considerably. The point upon which Paul insists is that the gifts are for the common good.

Some of the tensions and conflicts with which Paul is confronted in the Corinthian community are related to charisms. In spite of their disruptive nature, however, he does not attempt to repress them. What he offers is a vision of how they might be understood and fostered. Particular emphasis is given to those gifts that are able to build up the community. It is within this context that Paul inserts his famous hymn to love. It represents "the still more excellent way" that transcends all the gifts and without which they are of no avail (1 Cor 13:1-13).

The charisms to which the NT refers are often extraordinary. This is certainly the case in 1 Corinthians with its mention of tongues, healing, and the like. But even there a priority is given to those who are appointed apostles, prophets, and teachers. Included in the list of other gifts are "helpers" and "administrators." These more natural manifestations of the presence of the Spirit are emphasized in the parallel passage in Romans. There Paul refers to service, exhortation, the giving of aid, and acts of mercy. Vatican II states that "whether these charisms be very remarkable or more simple and widely diffused, they are to be received with thanksgiving and consolation"(*Lumen gentium* 12).

One of the more notable phenomena of the post-conciliar period, especially in the North American Church, was the development of the so-called charismatic or pentecostal movement. It dramatically called attention to the reality of the Spirit and the importance of his gifts. Like every such movement it had its difficulties and provoked negative as well as positive responses. In spite of the prayerfulness and the intimate community life that it fostered, many felt that it did a disservice by appropriating to itself the language of charism. Charisms are related to baptism and are present and active wherever authentic growth in the spiritual life takes place. They can be found throughout the

Church and in the most varied forms. The challenge for Church leaders is to discern and foster them.

Without charisms, no authentic Christian life or worship is possible. If they were to be totally absent, a parish or diocese would be a spiritual wasteland. Once again the basic norm was formulated by Paul: "Do not quench the Spirit, do not despise prophesying, but test everything; hold fast what is good, abstain from every form of evil" (1 Thess 5:19-22).

Central to Vatican II's view of the Church and certainly an implication of all the biblical images to which it appealed is the conviction that Church equals community. The considerable emphasis in the Catholic tradition since the medieval period on the hierarchy, an emphasis that the successive crises provoked by the Reformation and nineteenth century social and political change only reinforced, resulted in a tendency to identify the Church with its leadership. Although the development of the lay apostolate in the early part of this century went a certain distance in redressing the balance, it was only at the council that the shift in emphasis was clearly articulated.

In an early draft of *Lumen gentium* the order of the first three chapters was as follows: the mystery of the Church, the hierarchy, the people of God. The present text reverses the second and third chapters. The change was deliberate. The Church, the document insists, is the whole community. The ordained leadership is not the Church, nor should it even be thought of as being outside and above it. It exists *in* the Church as a ministry or service that is meant to help build it up. The great French Dominican ecclesiologist, Yves Congar, said soon after the council that it would take a generation or more before the attitudes and structures could be developed without which the word "in" here would have no meaning. The conflicts and failures of the post-conciliar period have made clear just how difficult the task is.

Vatican II accepted the traditional language for distinguishing between clergy and laity. Although almost everything in the first two chapters of *Lumen gentium* applies to both groups, chap. 4 of the same document deals specifically with the laity as does a separate decree on their apostolate. The emphasis at the council was on the role of the laity in the world. The argument was simple. If genuine inculturation of the gospel is to take place in modern secular society it will only do so if those who live in the structures of that society bring it about. The task is enormously complex and difficult and raises questions of the most fundamental nature. What does it mean today at all, for example, to bring a Christian perspective to politics and economics, to the media and social life? What, in particular, is implied when one attempts to do it in a pluralistic and largely secular environment? How can it be done in a way that respects the relative autonomy of the secular order? The answers to these and similar questions have varied dramatically. One need only think of the different approaches in Poland, Brazil, Nicaragua, the U.S., and Canada. What is remarkable about all these cases, and in some degree a measure of their success, is the role played in them by lay people of the most varied background.

A closely related theme and one that has considerable pastoral implications is that of the family as the domestic Church (*Lumen gentium* 11). Everything that is implied in the language of people of God, body of Christ, and temple of the Spirit, is meant to come alive first of all in the family. Ideally a community of reconciliation and of mutual forgiveness, it is there that faith and love are to be fostered and nourished. Nor can families do this in isolation. Families need other families.

A serious challenge facing contemporary Christianity is to make the gospel come alive in the concreteness of everyday life. In order in the modern world to believe its message at all, people need to have some experience of its healing and renewing power. This is one of the reasons why base communities or other small groups have taken on such significance. It is only in such contexts that the notion of Christian community begins to become real. One has the impression that only those parishes are really alive where families and other small groups take an active part in the development of their own faith life.

If Vatican II emphasized the role of the laity in the world, the post-conciliar period has been characterized by the development of various lay ministries in the Church. The more visible examples here have been their roles as lectors and as ministers of communion. Some lay people have become involved on a fulltime basis whether in parishes or as chaplains in hospitals, prisons or other institutions. In order to provide some kind of continuing structure for the conciliar emphasis on co-responsibility, many parishes and dioceses have established pastoral councils of various kinds. The fact that these have not been more successful reflects the difficulty clergy and laity alike have experienced in overcoming the attitudes of the past.

One of the more striking aspects of lay involvement at the present time in North America is in the area of theology. In recent decades increasing numbers of the laity, including sisters, have taken courses and completed degrees. Many lay people are now teaching the various theological disciplines in Catholic seminaries and faculties as well as in public and private universities. What this has created is a substantial resource for Church life and renewal. Such people bring a life experience and a sensitivity which are different from those of the clergy. A comparison of those who are presently studying and teaching theology with the situation on the eve of the council is as dramatic an example as any of the changes that have taken place.

If what has just been said is true of the laity in general, it is even more true of women. A growing percentage of teachers as well as students in Catholic faculties of theology are women. For the first time the perspectives and the concerns of women are being brought into theology itself. This in turn has become a source of stimulation and nourishment for women in the Church at large.

Although media attention has focused on the ordination issue, the presence of women in the theological community has succeeded in raising awareness about the many subtle and not so subtle attitudes and practices that have undermined their contribution in the past. A key notion here is patriarchy. The concept is descriptive of certain types of culture. Just as the Church was influenced by the philosophy and religious practices of the Hellenistic world, so also and inevitably it took on aspects of the patriarchal cultures within which it lived. The challenge here as in the earlier case is to discern what the gospel itself is saying from the ways in which its message has become confused with, or distorted by, mentalities that in many cases are at odds with it.

In order for Vatican II's vision of the Church to be effective, a great deal of effort will have to be made by every level to insure that the dignity and rights of women are respected in practice as well as in theory. Given the past, this will require from many an intellectual and moral conversion. If such a conversion does not take place, not only will women feel more and more alienated from the community of faith, but the Church's own efforts to defend human dignity and human rights in the world at large will lose credibility.

The language of Christ as priest, prophet, and king or shepherd is fundamental to the whole of Vatican II's ecclesiology. All three titles are biblical in origin. They are, of course, not the only ways in which the NT speaks of Jesus nor are they necessarily the most helpful ones for today. The Constitution on the Church in the Modern World, for example, calls him the perfect human being who cannot help but make those who approach him more human. In medieval and even more in Reformation theology, the language of priest, prophet and king became a focused way of summing up what was called the office of Christ. Repeated recourse is had to this language at Vatican II to suggest some of the implications of the fact that to be Christian is to be in Christ and to share in his life and mission. The Church, as the body of Christ and as the community animated by his Spirit, participates in his threefold office. This is true of Church leadership, but it is also true of the community at large.

At the time of the Reformation Luther rejected the priestly interpretation of the ordained ministry and insisted upon the priesthood of all believers. His preferred text in this regard is one that was cited in chapter one, 1 Pet 2:1-10. Parts of the same text are referred to several times in the documents of Vatican II. Although the council insists that "the common priesthood of the faithful and the ministerial or hierarchical priesthood" "differ essentially and not only in degree" *(Lumen gentium* 10), the return of the concept of the priesthood of the faithful to the forefront of ecclesiology provides a way of articulating the dignity and importance of all members of the community of faith. It is this common priesthood that most profoundly identifies believers with Christ and that undergirds the whole process of growth into his likeness. Because his priesthood was exercised not in the temple but in the concreteness of everyday life, it had a decidedly non-cultic, even lay, character about it. Faith, obedience, and self-giving love were at the heart of both his sacrifice and his priesthood. The same is true in regard to the priesthood of the faithful. It is the quality of one's Christian life that is the measure of one's sharing in that priesthood. The Christian cult involves both explicit acts of worship and a life lived according to the Spirit of Jesus. The whole sacramental system from this perspective is a means to an end. In so far as Church office can be understood in priestly terms, it is clearly ministerial in nature. It is meant to serve and to foster the priesthood of all believers.

The language of prophecy is used at Vatican II to underline the crucial function played by the whole community in the preservation and handling on of the gospel message. Recalling a widely held conviction of the medieval Church, it asserts that "the whole body of the faithful who have an anointing that comes from the holy one (cf. 1 Jn 2:20, 27), cannot err in matters of faith" *(Lumen gentium* 12). This echoes the teaching of Vatican I which affirmed that the pope is the organ and the instrument of the infallibility with which Christ willed to endow his Church.

The sharing of all Christians in the prophetic office of Christ is a factor in the development of doctrine *(Lumen gentium* 12 and the Constitution on Revelation 8). The prayer, reflection, and life-experience of the whole community contribute to a growing and deepening insight into the meaning of the gospel and its implications for a given age. Here again, as important as the role of the teaching authority within the Church is, it will only be effective when it is open to, and in dialogue with, the insights, concerns, and experiences of all the faithful.

Prophecy in the Catholic tradition is related to the theme of witness. The prophetic gift is one that makes the word and the voice of God present in human life. This has been over the centuries one of the great contributions of the saints. Their lives have suggested ways in which the gospel could be made incarnate in their time. As with the prophets of old, such lives have been both a consolation and a challenge. If the role of the saints is unique, all Christians are called according to their gifts to live the gospel in their own situations and thus provide the witness and the vitality without which the life of the Church would soon wither.

The ways in which all believers share in Christ's kingship are less clearly spelled out. In the liturgical tradition the theme of kingship has surfaced as an expression for the special dignity that is bestowed on them in baptism.

Although kingship is related to the messianic idea, it is perhaps not the best way to formulate this aspect of Christ's role. In the NT itself Jesus is clearly not a king in any ordinary sense. The image that is more often used and which is closer to the concrete form of his mission, is that of shepherd. It too has roots in the Hebrew tradition where it is applied both to God and to various leaders of the people. In the NT Jesus is the good shepherd who lays down his life for his sheep. Leaders of the community are encouraged to model themselves on his example.

Within the context of a contemporary ecclesiology the language of shepherd suggests that as in the case of the priestly and prophetic offices all believers share in Christ's pastoral function. Although their responsibilities in this regard are not the same as those of the ordained, they are none the less real and none the less essential for the well-being of the Church. One need only think here of the role that parents play in regard to children or teachers to students. The same obviously applies to counselling and to the whole range of activities related to the care of the poor and the sick. At times spouses exercise a genuinely pastoral role in their relationships to one another, as do friends. Everywhere Christians reach out a hand of support or offer a word of hope and encouragement, Christ the shepherd is present among his people guiding them to the fulness of life.

There is a sense in which all believers share a co-responsibility for the pastoral oversight of the Church. If this flows from the laity's participation in the shepherding function of Christ, it is also implicit in the extension in the years since the council of the notion of collegiality beyond the bishops to embrace the whole community. The challenge here as elsewhere is to develop the structures that will enable them to play their role. What is required are not only parish and diocesan pastoral councils but also periodic diocesan and national synods.

This rapid reflection on the participation of all believers in the threefold office of Christ suggests one way that contemporary Catholic theology uses in order to emphasize the dignity of the laity and the importance of their active involvement in all aspects of Church life. Another way and one that fits into a typically Catholic understanding of Christianity, has been to emphasize the sacraments of initiation and in particular to call attention to their ecclesial dimension. If the Church is the sacrament of Christ and his Spirit, then the individual sacraments are moments of special intensity in its life, moments in which it brings its inner resources to bear on individuals either entering or already within the community.

An earlier approach to baptism stressed its negative effects. It was seen above all as taking away original sin. The emphasis now is more positive; it is also more communitarian. Baptism is a rite of initiation, a way by which a person becomes a member of the community of faith. The process has both individual and social implications. One enters into the Church in the very act by which one is plunged into the dying and rising of Christ and receives the gift of his Spirit.

The Rite of Christian Initiation of Adults (RCIA) has helped to bring back an awareness of the baptismal practice of the early Church. Because adult baptism was then the norm, personal faith and conversion were demanded before the sacrament could be administered. In the first centuries it was regularly celebrated within the liturgical assembly of an already existing community into which the newly baptized were then welcomed. The all but universal practice of infant baptism in later periods undermined for many people a sense of all that was implied in the rite in terms of both gift and commitment. The drama that originally accompanied the entry into the community came to be transferred to religious life or to ordination. Modern secularism has once again made faith and Church membership much less obvious than they once were. Here, the RCIA could help to recapture something of what is involved in adult faith. Its demand for an active participation in the initiation process by the receiving parish is a forceful reminder that authentic Christian life is only possible within a community that nourishes and supports it.

In antiquity confirmation or chrismation was part of the rite of initiation. In the Western Church it became separated from that rite and took on the form that we now know. Theology has always tried to relate this sacrament in some way to Christian maturity. The current debates as to when it should be conferred point to a renewed sense of its importance. It is now seen in close relationship to baptism. Both sacraments together proclaim the dignity of believers and challenge them to assume a mature and active role in the life and mission of the Church.

The third of the sacraments of initiation is the eucharist. At one time baptism and confirmation, ordinarily celebrated together at the Easter vigil, led immediately to a sharing in the eucharist. This is once again the case with the RCIA. The eucharist, however, is more than a sacrament of initiation. It is *the* sacrament *par excellence*, the central religious act of the Church, one in which much of what is essential to its life and mission is both expressed and renewed.

Reflection on the relationship between the Church and the eucharist that was begun by Paul in 1 Corinthians continued throughout the patristic and medieval periods. On the one hand, the Church was thought to exist primarily in order to celebrate the eucharist and in so doing to offer praise and thanks to God and to make memory of his saving act in Christ's death and resurrection. On the other hand, the eucharist was understood as the primary means by which the risen Christ, through his Spirit, continued to nourish and build up his Church. The individual themes here are too many to go into in detail. The self-giving of Jesus that is celebrated and rendered present is the model and the source of Christian discipleship; the sharing by all present in the one bread and the one cup is meant to deepen their relationship to Christ and to one another; thanksgiving and praise are the fundamental obligation of a community the whole life of which depends on gift, the once and for all gift of the life of Jesus and the continuing gift of his Spirit.

One of the major reasons for recent changes in the eucharistic liturgy, from the use of the vernacular to the involvement of lay people as readers and ministers of communion, has been to facilitate the development of a sense that the eucharist is a community activity, that it is a celebration of, and a means for renewing, the whole Church.

The central ecclesiological affirmation of Vatican II is that the Church is a community of believers. This is clearly affirmed by the great biblical images of the people of God, the body of Christ, and the temple of the Spirit. All the faithful and not just the ordained share in the threefold office of Christ. Everyone who is baptized and confirmed is called to maturity and co-responsibility within the community.

At its deepest level the Church is rooted in, and is carried by, the mystery of the triune God. Its being and mission are related to creation as well as to redemption. Founded on the event of Christ it lives out of the renewing presence in it of his Spirit.

4

Structuring The Community Of Faith

The Church was never an amorphous community. From the beginning it had, at least in a rudimentary fashion, what one might call an official ministry. The most obvious and important form of this in the period immediately following the resurrection was the apostolic office. No matter how precisely this was understood, it was agreed that the word and witness of the apostles had called the Church into being. For this they were remembered and cherished. There was a widespread sense that the new community was "built upon the foundation of the apostles and prophets, Christ Jesus himself being the cornerstone" (Eph 2:20).

As local communities sprang up in response to the spread of the gospel they were given or created for themselves some kind of basic structure. Someone had to assume responsibility for those things without which there could be no Church. It has already been shown that development in this area was slow and that it often differed from one community to another. By the beginning of the second century a pattern had been established that would become traditional, the threefold division of the ordained ministry into bishops, presbyters and deacons. Before long each local Church was led by a single bishop. Because initially the communities were small the bishop himself was able to preside at all their major liturgical celebrations including baptism and the eucharist. In this period the presbyters probably functioned as a council of elders supporting and giving advice to the bishop. With continued growth and expansion some of the bishop's functions were taken over by them. The deacons, on the other hand, remained close collaborators of the bishop particularly in regard to his charitable and social responsibilities.

Problems relating to unity have been with the Church since the beginning. In spite of the pluralism that is such a marked feature of the NT, its individual writings reveal a considerable concern for unity both among the local Churches and within them. In the account of the early period in Acts the Jerusalem Church fulfilled a special function in this regard. The story of the so-called council of Jerusalem tells how unity was maintained on the crucial issue of the demands that were to be made of Gentile converts. In the concern that Paul's letters reflect for the poor in Jerusalem, one can recognize his desire to bind newly founded Churches to the original community.

Because faith was so fundamental a reality and because it had a specific object in the person and life of Jesus, questions and controversies arose about it and its formulation from the outset. One senses this in almost every book of the NT. Although there is considerable creativity in the early period there is also a deep concern to defend the gospel against misunderstandings and distortions. Paul's letter to the Galatians is eloquent in this regard: "If anyone is preaching to you a gospel contrary to that which you received, let him be accursed" (Gal 1:9). The letters to Timothy and Titus reflect a situation towards the end of the first century. By this time false teaching and vain speculation are threatening to undermine the community and to cause individuals to shipwreck. Timothy is admonished to "have nothing to do with stupid, senseless controversies" (2 Tim 2:23). His pastoral responsibilities are recalled in a solemn charge: "preach the word, be urgent in season and out of season, convince, rebuke, and exhort, be unfailing in patience and in teaching. For the time is coming when people will not endure sound teaching, but having itching ears they will accumulate for themselves teachers to suit their own likings, and will turn away from listening to the truth and wander into myths" (2 Tim 4:2-4).

There is an inherent tension in all efforts to formulate the content of faith. If the gospel is going to be able to speak to and challenge different cultural situations and peoples, there has to be some flexibility in the way it is understood. Too great a flexibility, however, could led to its dissolution. In its first several centuries the Church was blessed with remarkably gifted bishops and theologians who were able successfully to bring the gospel into a positive and yet critical relation with the Hellenistic world. This historic achievement was not attained without conflict and division. Some Christians, for example, adopted positions that were clearly imcompatible with the gospel. It was in part to meet the challenge that this represented that emphasis was given to what came to be called the apostolic tradition and to more and more precise creedal formulations. Irenaeus, a late second century bishop and martyr, developed most consistently an understanding of the role of the bishop as a public teacher within the Church whose task it was to maintain and defend the revealed word such as it was expressed in the Scriptures and handed down in the tradition of the Church.

It was also in the second century that bishops from Churches in a given region began to meet together at what were called synods in order to deal with issues of common concern. At the beginning of the fourth century, the Emperor Constantine convened at Nicaea what turned out to be the first ecumenical council. Here was a development that would make history. Such councils became key instruments for maintaining and developing what the pastoral letters had referred to as "sound doctrine" but which by now was known as "orthodoxy."

In the first centuries of Christianity, the basic unit of the Church was what came to be called the diocese. It was an area over which a single bishop exercised leadership. In some ways, all dioceses were equal; in others, they were not. From the beginning a special significance was given to those Churches that were thought to have been founded by the apostles. Later there developed the notion of patriarchal sees. Churches like those of Rome, Alexandria, Antioch, and Jerusalem exerted a certain dominance over the areas in which they were located. The claims of these particular Churches were obvious. The first three were the great cities of the empire while the fourth was the Holy City itself. Peter was believed to be tied up in some way with them all including Alexandria. After the seat of the emperor was shifted to Constantinople it too took on patriarchal status.

The early Church thrived on pluralism. The patriarchal sees in particular represented differing liturgical and theological emphases. Because there was no central bureaucracy or common code of canon law, the unity that was experienced had nothing to do with uniformity. It was more like a communion or fellowship of various Churches. Their common bond was fostered by letters and visits and by the developing practice of local and ecumenical councils.

From the second century various Churches appealed to Rome for support or to ask for help in resolving local difficulties. The bishops of Rome for their part did not hesitate to intervene on occasion in the inner life of other Churches including those in the East. In the eyes of the Roman Church its growing importance was tied up with the role ascribed to Peter in the NT. The fact that it was the only apostolic see and the only patriarchal Church in the Latin-speaking West gave it an ascendancy in that region from a very early date.

One of the tragic facts of the history of the Church was that as the ancient world collapsed the Eastern and Western halves of Christianity drifted apart until to a large degree their medieval experiences took place in reciprocal isolation. This had a profound effect on the way that the role of the bishop of Rome came to be exercised and understood in Latin Christianity.

The history of the papacy is both long and complex. In the medieval period it was involved in almost every aspect of society and culture. Its conflicts and struggles with feudal kings and emperors were not only major events in the world of that time but they helped to give concrete form to the papal office and to determine its mode of acting even within the Church. It was not by chance that the first treatises on ecclesiology were written by canon lawyers in the eleventh and twelfth centuries and that they bore such titles as "On the Power of the Papacy" and "On the Authority of the Roman Church."

From the eleventh century on, the pope became a progressively more dominant figure in the life of the Western Church. In terms of spiritual authority the development reached a climax with the definition of papal primacy and infallibility at Vatican I in 1870. In the intervening period there was considerable opposition to the course that the development was taking. It came from various spiritual and conciliarist movements in the medieval period, from the Protestant Reformation, and from the claims of Gallicanism and other Catholic national Churches in the seventeenth and eighteenth centuries. In the end the opposition had little effect. The final result of this whole history was the markedly Romecentered emphasis that was so distinctive a feature of the Catholic community in the period leading up to Vatican II. A centralized bureaucracy in the Curia, a common code of canon law and the use of Latin in theology and liturgy reinforced the dominant position that Rome had come to assume. There were, of course, other Churches from the East in union with Rome, but their presence was unable to change the over-all picture. The Catholic Church, in spite of all its national differences and the multiplicity of its religious orders, was a communion in which at some levels at least unity was interpreted as uniformity.

Given this background, the very fact of convening an ecumenical council was bound to have a profound effect. It reawakened a sense of what is called the conciliar principle and prompted theologians and historians to look again at the whole of Church history in order better to understand the balance and interplay that should exist between pope and bishops, Rome and the local Churches, unity and diversity. At Vatican II, as already indicated above, the debate about these issues took place primarily around the notion of collegiality. Although in no way intending to undermine the authority and office of the pope, the council affirmed the co-responsibility of the bishops with him for the well-being of the universal Church.

A theme that was closely related to, and implicit in, discussions of collegiality was the theme of Catholicity. The word Catholic means universal. Although initially used in the patristic period to distinguish the large Church from heretical sects, it soon took on a qualitative meaning. It referred to a fundamental openness and readiness to embrace all that was true and good wherever it might be found. Such an attitude entails a certain pluralism; it affirms the importance of a truly indigenous local Church.

[margin note: catholic]

The term local Church is understood in different ways. Sometimes it refers to a single diocese and sometimes to groupings of several dioceses. In the early centuries there were intermediary levels of various kinds between the diocese and the universal Church at which significant collaboration took place. The tendency to work together in this way was reinforced by the distinctive theological and liturgical traditions that marked various ethnic and linguistic areas. In the period leading up to Vatican II some national episcopates had begun to cooperate in new ways. What was thus begun received a tremendous impulse from the conciliar experience as well as from discussions about collegiality.

Some of the most striking developments of the post-conciliar period have been related to the notion of the local Church in the broad sense. National hierarchies organized themselves in order to implement more effectively the council's decisions. There was a widespread conviction in many countries that more adaptation had to be made to local traditions and experiences. Given the pre-conciliar emphasis on uniformity and centralization it was inevitable that this enthusiastic rediscovery of the local Church would be accompanied by conflict and tension. This was very much the case with the Church of Holland. Rome itself intervened in its inner life in an effort to rein in what it considered to be excessively centrifugal forces. In Canada and the United States the process developed at a more steady pace. The national organizations in both countries have been effective in adapting catechetical and liturgical material to their respective Churches. Both national bodies have been in the forefront of those attempting to articulate local implications of general Catholic teaching on issues of justice and peace. The meetings of the Latin American bishops at Medellin and Puebla were historic moments in the development of a consciousness of a Latin American Church. They represent key steps in the process by which the vision of the council came to be adapted to the Latin American world. The attempts by some of the Churches in that world to deal with the intractable economic and social problems of their areas have been nothing short of heroic.

The growing awareness of local Churches and of their responsibility to translate the gospel and the teachings of the universal Church into their own situation is clearly the direction of the future. The task, however, is not a simple one. It inevitably involves a good deal of trial and error. This has led some people to lament what has taken place and to call for a return to an earlier practice. Recent tensions between Rome and the Church of Brazil over liberation theology as well as the difficulties experienced by the Archbishop of Seattle are typical of the problems that this kind of development entails. The fact that in both of these cases an initial attitude or action of Rome was modified suggests that ways were found in which the concerns of both local and central authorities came to be heard and respected. That the cases arose at all underlines the need to develop procedures that will do justice in such situations to all the parties and all the principles involved.

The actual experience of Vatican II was such a positive one that Paul VI was anxious to continue it in some way. He instituted the practice of holding synods to which representative bishops from around the world would come approximately every three years to discuss matters of common concern. Until now these synods have been consultative and not legislative. They make suggestions to the pope, but it is entirely up to him to decide what he should do with them. A number of bishops over the years have stated their conviction that the synods would be more effective instruments of collegiality if they were given the power to decide and to act as well as to discuss. In spite of this weakness the synods have filled an important function. The simple fact that bishops from different countries meet periodically helps them to think more spontaneously in terms of the world Church. They learn from one another and in the process contribute to the building up of a common consciousness. The 1971 synod on social justice, for example, was the occasion for a deepened appreciation by North American bishops of the Latin American situation and in particular of the significance of liberation theology.

The extraordinary synod of 1985 referred explicitly to the value of such shared experiences. It also spoke of the importance of collegiality. Although it recognized that the highest form of collegial action is an ecumenical council, it affirmed that such things as the synod of bishops and episcopal conferences can also be important instruments for the development and expression of the collegial spirit. Because "the episcopal conferences are so useful, indeed necessary, in the present day pastoral work of the Church," it called for a serious study of their "theological 'status,'" an idea about which there is currently some debate.

If the new emphases at Vatican II were on the bishops and, by implication, on national Churches, the idea was never to oppose them to the papal office. The Petrine ministry is essential to the Catholic understanding of Christianity. Recent ecumenical discussions have shown that Anglicans, Lutherans, and others are willing to think about some form of such a ministry in a future united Church. There it would function as a sign and instrument of unity. It could also serve as a safeguard against any tendency to retreat into ecclesial nationalism. One of the strengths of the Roman Catholic Church is that it is to such a degree a world wide community. The problems of the Churches of Africa, the Philippines, Latin America, and Eastern Europe should be part of the concerns of Catholics in North America. The Petrine office is a major factor in reminding Catholics of their brothers and sisters everywhere and of their responsibilities to them and to their societies.

The actual working of the papacy involves a great deal more than the person of the pope. An important element here is the Roman Curia with its various offices or congregations and secretariats. It is the oldest bureaucracy in the Western world with roots that reach far back into the medieval period. Its mode and scope of activity have changed with the times. They are influenced by political and cultural situations as well as by such concrete things as the means of travel and of communication. Revolutions in these latter areas are opening up the possibility of far more extensive consultation than ever before.

The way in which popes have related concretely to the Church has varied over the centuries. John Paul II, for example, continuing a practice begun by Paul VI, has taken advantage of the possibilities offered by jet travel and by television. He has become a kind of wandering preacher, going from country to country, proclaiming the message of the gospel. Some of his trips have generated an atmosphere analogous to that of a revival meeting. It is indicative that the present pope's favorite NT text in regard to his office is not Matthew's "Thou art Peter and upon this rock I will build my church," but rather the phrase in Luke's account of the last supper, "I have prayed for you that your faith may not fail; and when you have turned again, strengthen your brethren" (Lk 22:32). It is the desire to be of help and strengthen the local Church that motivates most of his trips. This, he believes, is an important aspect of collegiality.

The continued reception of Vatican II as well as the ongoing ecumenical dialogue will keep alive in the Church a sense of the need to balance within its institutional structures both the episcopal and the papal ministries. Both are of the essence of the Church. History teaches that it is not easy to maintain a balance between them. The temptation in the future as in the past will be to insist on one at the expense of the other. It is a temptation that will have to be courageously resisted.

In the years immediately following the council, there were those who said that Vatican II, with its concern for bishops and the laity, had all but forgotten the priests. On occasion this was even brought forward as one of the reasons why so many priests were leaving the active ministry and why vocations dropped so precipitously. People spoke of an identity crisis on the part of the clergy. Whatever precise effect the council and its teaching had on priests, it is certain that what happened to them in the late 60's and early 70's was due to many factors both in and outside the Church. What is important to note is that the council did in fact say a great deal about priests and what it said pointed in new directions. What is obvious, however, is that the new vision was neither fully worked out nor consistently presented.

At the council of Trent the fundamental category for understanding the ordained ministry was that of priesthood or *sacerdotium*. The presentation on ordination began by affirming that in his relation to humankind God had always seen to it that there would be an official priesthood. And so it was that as a parallel to the Levitical priesthood of Israel Jesus at the last supper ordained the apostles priests *(sacerdotes)* and entrusted to them the sacrifice of the eucharist. Although Trent was deeply interested in the renewal of the spiritual life of bishops and priests and although it was perfectly aware of the importance to their office of preaching and teaching, in its dogmatic formulations it emphasized exclusively the power that is conferred by ordination and in virtue of which priests are able "to confect the eucharist and to forgive sins."

This approach to the ordained ministry goes back to the medieval period and can only be understood in relation to the development of sacramental theology at that time and to the then new practice of ordaining monks without any pastoral responsibility. This resulted in what has to be described from the perspective of the NT as a one-sided understanding of ecclesial office. It was against this one-sided understanding that Luther and the other reformers reacted, and it was against their reactions that Trent formulated its own position. Historical research has shown that the desire at that time was not to offer a balanced view of the ordained ministry, but to affirm those elements of the Catholic tradition that were being denied. Unfortunately this historical context tended subsequently to be lost sight of, and the doctrinal statements of Trent were taken as offering an adequate basis on which to develop a theology of the priesthood.

By the time of Vatican II Catholic theologians were beginning to turn directly to the NT for inspiration. What struck them there in regard to the present topic was that the language of priesthood was all but totally absent in references to Church leaders of whatever kind. Although it was applied to Christ in Hebrews and to the whole community in passages like 1 Pet 2:1-10, it does not figure among the many titles used for Church leaders. These were called pastors and teachers, overseers (*episcopoi*) and elders (*presbyteroi*), deacons and apostles. The one text that has priestly connotations underlines the way all such terminology was understood to have been transformed by the person and mission of Jesus.

Near the end of Romans Paul speaks of the grace given him by God "to be a minister of Christ Jesus to the Gentiles in the priestly service of the gospel of God, so that the offering of the Gentiles may be acceptable, sanctified by the Holy Spirit" (Rom 15:16). The Greek word translated here as "the priestly service" comes from a verb meaning to act as a priest. Paradoxically what in the text is called a "priestly service" is the preaching of the gospel. What this refers to is the fact that by preaching Paul invites and exhorts people to the kind of faith and life that constitute what Ephesians calls "a fragrant offering and sacrifice to God" (Eph 5:2). Everything that in any way helps people to live in Christ and according to his Spirit is in this sense a priestly act.

Conscious of the NT data the framers of Vatican II's major document on priests are careful in most instances to use the word *presbyter* rather than *sacerdos* in referring to them. Those who wrote the decree on preparation for the priestly office were much less careful. An already complex theological point is made even more confusing by the fact that the standard English translations of Vatican II employ "priest" for both *presbyter* and *sacerdos*.

Is all this just a matter of words? Not at all. Priest in the sense of *sacerdos* is clearly a cultic term. It evokes temple and sacrifice. Used of the Christian ministry it invites parallels with the priesthood of the OT. Historically this language has reinforced a tendency in the Catholic tradition to think of the ordained minister as someone set apart, a sacred figure not really at home in the secular world, and this in a way quite different from all other Christians. The fact that celibacy was made a mandatory condition for ordination reinforced and gave forceful expression to this point of view. The NT word *presbyteros,* on the other hand, means an elder and when used to describe an office or function has lay connotations. In Judaism elders were associated with the synagogue and not the temple. Theirs was a responsibility of oversight.

The ordained ministry in the NT and early Church was never understood exclusively or even primarily in terms of sacramental power. It was first of all a pastoral task involving in a special way responsibility for teaching and preaching. It entailed community leadership including the gathering together and leading of the community in prayer and worship. Initially the office was not seen as demanding a totally different way of life with special requirements such as celibacy. The emphasis in fact was on being a model and pattern for all the believers.

Vatican II tried to recapture something of all this by its use of the language of presbyter and by its insistence on the pastoral nature of all ordained ministry. By way of contrast with the post-Tridentine emphasis it affirmed that the first responsibility of presbyters is the preaching of the gospel.

Presbyters as well as bishops share in the threefold office of Christ, priest, prophet and shepherd, although they do this in the Catholic tradition at a lower level of the hierarchy. Presbyters are collaborators of the bishop and are required to cooperate with him in his leadership of the local diocese. Bishops, on the other hand, are encouraged to respect them as associates in a common task and to seek their advice and counsel in the fulfillment of their responsibilities.

Vatican II emphasized the importance of the presbyterium. Just as bishops are not to think of themselves in isolation but as members of a college having co-responsibility for the universal Church, so also presbyters in a particular diocese belong to a corporate body called the presbyterium. As such, they have a responsibility that reaches beyond their immediate duties to embrace the diocese as a whole. The senates and councils of priests that have been set up since the council are meant to foster this idea and to provide it with an instrument for becoming a reality.

An issue that the bishops were not allowed to address in any detail at the council, the mandatory celibacy of the clergy, became a focus of concern in the post-conciliar period. There is no historical or theological necessity for bishops and presbyters to be celibate. It was not the case in the NT, nor was it widely practiced in the first several centuries. In the Eastern Church a distinction was made between monks and the leaders of local communities. The latter, with the exception of the bishops, were not required to be celibate. Some, of course, were, but most married before being ordained. In the West the tradition took another turn. By the medieval period it was taken for granted that anyone in major orders would be a celibate. From the eleventh century on the attempted marriage of such a person was automatically invalid.

The contemporary debate has focused on the shortage of the clergy as well as on the importance of having in the ranks of bishops and presbyters people with a married as well as a celibate experience. This latter point seems to be particularly pressing at a time when the pastoral challenges in regard to marriage and family life are so acute. What some believe is called for is a two-pronged renewal. On the one hand, religious communities have to be encouraged to continue to renew themselves from their roots and to recommit themselves to the authentic charism of their founders and traditions. Such communities should be the favored contexts for fostering the charism of celibacy. It seems clear that in the foreseeable future such life will be for the few. On the other hand, the secular clergy could well benefit from including in its ranks married as well as single people. Realistically this would bring new problems and necessitate wide-ranging changes, but in spite of that it seems to be the direction in which the Church is being called.

There is an obvious sense in which the ordaining of married men in the secular clergy would be within the logic of Vatican II. The council consciously began the process of moving beyond the one-sided emphases of the post-Reformation period. It did this by returning to an earlier moment in the Church's history, a moment marked by a less sectarian and more authentically Catholic spirit. And so the council emphasized both word and sacrament, both Scripture and tradition. In an analogous way the great Catholic tradition, embracing both East and West, antiquity and modernity, surely has room for an ordained ministry that would include the married as well as the single.

A step was taken in this direction by the decision to ordain married men as deacons. This decision not only opened one of the major orders to those who are married, it also revived as a separate ministry what for centuries in the West had been little more than a steppingstone to the presbyterate.

In terms of numbers the restoration of the diaconate has been a notable success. There remain, however, debates about the precise meaning of the permanent diaconate. Some have emphasized its liturgical side while others have insisted on its service-oriented functions. In these latter areas the fact of ordination has given a heightened ecclesial visibility to many social and pastoral activities that were already being undertaken. The most ambivalent aspect of the whole program has been the use that some would like to make of it as a stopgap for dealing with the shortage of the clergy. The problem with such efforts is that if successful they would result in a separation of the sacramental from the pastoral aspects of the episcopal and presbyteral ministries. Such a separation would in the long run be disastrous both for those immediately involved and for the community at large.

The question of the ordination of women has come to the fore within the Roman Catholic Church relatively recently. For most Catholics, including most bishops, the idea was all but inconceivable at the time of the council. It was not debated then because it was not even raised. The fact that it is now is due in part to the new atmosphere created by the women's movement and in part to the general openness fostered by the council itself. *Gaudium et spes* included the women's movement as one of the signs of the times to which Church people have to be attentive. That, plus an acute sense of the historically conditioned nature of so many of the Church's structures and attitudes, led a growing number of people in North America and Western Europe to question why women could not be ordained.

In 1977 the Congregation for the Doctrine of the Faith published a statement on the issue. That it did so at all was a sign of how far the movement had come. The basic argument of the Congregation was that the hands of Church authorities were tied. The practice of Jesus and the unbroken tradition in this regard created a sign of divine intention against which the pope and bishops could not act. A secondary argument attempted to give reasons why this was the case.

According to the document, there is a particular fittingness that males should be priests because in certain of their functions priests act in the person of Christ. The fulness of the symbolism would be lost in the case of a female. Whatever the other issues raised by this argument, what provoked the strongest reaction was the implication that women qua women are incapable of fully imaging Christ.

Although some theologians rallied to defend the positions adopted by the document, many more rejected them. The Catholic Theological Society of America set up a committee to review the arguments and to write a theological response. Its conclusion, like the conclusions of many individual theologians, was that there are no convincing theological reasons in either Scripture or tradition that would rule out the possibility of ordaining women. There are on the contrary cultural, moral, and theological reasons why it should be seriously considered at the present time. A factor that complicates the discussion is that the cultural situation of women in Latin America, Africa, and the Orient has not undergone the same change that it has in the West. This creates a difficulty within a world-wide Church. Another factor is the ecumenical one. If the ordination of women is already an established fact in the Anglican and many Protestant communities, it is viewed as a theological impossibility in the Orthodox Churches. Insofar as Rome has hopes for organic unity with these Churches by the turn of the millenium, it will be even less open to the possibility of women's ordination than it might otherwise have been.

John Paul II broached the theme of the ordination of women during his first trip to the U. S. in 1979. He mentioned it in the context of a talk on the priesthood at Philadelphia, a talk in which he drew a parallel between the priestly and the prophetic vocations. To recall this parallel, he said, "should help us, too, to understand that the Church's traditional decision to call men to the priesthood, and not to call women, is not a statement about human rights, nor an exclusion of women from holiness and mission in the Church. Rather this decision expresses the conviction of the Church about this particular dimension of the gift of priesthood by which God has chosen to shepherd his flock." There is no mention here of whether or not women can image

Christ, nor even of divine law. Everything is made to depend upon vocation, upon God's calling of people to serve in this way. Paradoxically this leaves the question open in regard to the future. One thing that the history of the prophets teaches is that God's call is often surprising and unexpected. From this perspective, the task facing the Church is one of discernment. The whole community, together with it leaders, is challenged to listen intently to what God is saying to it through the signs of the time.

Reference has already been made to the symbolic importance of the reversal of the order of chapters 2 and 3 of *Lumen gentium*. The earlier order, the hierarchy and then the people of God, corresponds to a one-sidedly hierarchical view of the Church, a view that was reinforced by the political and social conditions of feudal and monarchical Europe. In such societies everything flowed from the top to the bottom. In the Church this meant from the pope through the bishops to the priests and finally to the laity. By reversing the chapters the bishops were calling for a new understanding of the relationship of the ordained ministry to the community as a whole. To suggest what this might be, they appealed to the biblical notion of *diakonia*.

If traditional ecclesiology evoked the image of a pyramid, the present approach suggests a circle. The Church is a community all the members of which are called through baptism and confirmation to play an active role. The Spirit of Christ is poured out on everyone, giving to each some share in his gifts. Those who are ordained were and remain members of this community and share in all aspects of its life and mission. By accepting ordination, which is itself a charism, they accept to offer a service of leadership. One of its main responsibilities is to call out and foster the gifts of others.

A basic task of the ordained ministry is to be a focus of unity. In this context, however, unity must not be understood statically but dynamically. It has to be pursued and built up. Its deepest roots are to be found within the divine unity itself. The more individuals are grounded in, and taken over by, Christ and his Spirit, the more profoundly they are united with one another. The ordained serve this unity by preaching the gospel and by leading people by word and example into the experience of the divine mystery. The sacraments represent special moments in the process. Although this is true of all the sacraments, it is especially true of the eucharist.

It is at the eucharist that much of what the Church is all about becomes visible. It is also in the eucharist that the varied strands of the pastoral office are drawn together. In the renewed liturgy, stress is placed upon the proclamation of the word and upon the homily that is meant to help people understand its implications for contemporary life. Here is a fundamental responsibility of all bishops and presbyters. They are to be people of the word, preachers and teachers, who are able to stimulate and nourish faith. They are also to be people of prayer, people who can, without hypocrisy, lead the community in asking for forgiveness and help and especially in the great hymn of praise and thanksgiving that constitutes the basic form of the eucharistic liturgy. Within that hymn memory is made of the life, death, and resurrection of Jesus. Through the power of the Spirit what is remembered is rendered present and becomes the food of life.

From start to finish the eucharist is a community act. All are invited to pray, to celebrate, to make memory, to share in the one bread. Nor is the healing power of the eucharist only directed at the individual; it is also meant to deepen community. In this regard the third canon is eloquent; it prays that "we who are nourished by his body and blood, may be filled with his Holy Spirit and become one body, one spirit in Christ." One of the greatest challenges for those who preside at eucharistic celebrations is to help people translate this vision into everyday life.

Because laity and clergy in spite of all differences are so intimately related, a change in the understanding and attitudes of the one necessarily has implications for the understanding and attitudes of the other. Where the renewed vision of Vatican II has been realized both have undergone conversion. Where one or the other group has failed to do this, the results have been partial at best. Somehow both have to learn together as they work out their respective roles. It is only by cooperation that the common good will be served.

The ecclesiological emphases of Vatican II, if acted upon, are more than adequate to effect a genuine renewal of Church life. Because, however, efforts in this direction have led to conflict and tension, there is a desire for clear and simple principles that once accepted might facilitate the process. One such principle is that of subsidiarity. A part of Catholic social teaching since Leo XIII, it is related in some sense to contemporary notions of decentralization. If things can be done at a local level there is no need to appeal to a higher or more central government or authority to do them. The concern is that if people are not allowed and encouraged to do what they can, they will lose all sense of initiative and of responsibility.

Pius XII in 1946 first suggested that the principle might be applied within the Church. In the post-conciliar years it was brought into a fruitful relation to the notion of collegiality. The 1985 synod requested that a study be made of its possible implications for Church life.

The principle is not without a certain ambiguity. If it were evoked simply to determine which level of authority were finally responsible for decision-making in some area or other, that could have unfortunate consequences. Questions of ordaining women or of changing the law of celibacy, for example, clearly require the involvement of the whole Church including the pope. That, however, does not mean that local Churches and their leaders do not have the responsibility to examine such issues seriously. If after study and prayer the bishops of a country are convinced that a change in policy is required, then this conviction must be communicated forcefully and eloquently to those levels of authority where the decision is to be made.

If subsidiarity is understood primarily in terms of the need to involve people to the extent of their competence in the decisions affecting them, then it could be an excellent rule of thumb for deciding how many things might be done. It would, for example, at the very least justify a genuine consultation of representative members of a local Church in regard to the qualities required of a future bishop; it would encourage the involvement of teachers and educators in the writing of catechisms; it would empower episcopal conferences to deal with liturgical and other issues related to local cultures.

Subsidiarity or for that matter any other principle will be unable by itself to renew the Church. Given, however, an appreciation for the religious realities involved in all Christian life, it, like collegiality and co-responsibility, will be able to suggest ways in which the renewed and renewing vision of Vatican II can continue to be implemented.

5

The Church, The Churches, and The World

Near the end of chapter one of *Lumen gentium* is a phrase the exact meaning of which is difficult to discern. Containing a first overview of "the mystery of the Church," the chapter introduces a number of biblical images including those of the temple of the Spirit and the body of Christ. To underline that the Church involves both visible and invisible elements, both the presence of God's saving grace and a human organizational structure, an analogy is drawn between it and the incarnation. It is in this context that the affirmation is made that "this Church, constituted and organized as a society in the present world, subsists in the Catholic Church, which is governed by the successor of Peter and by the bishops in communion with him" (*Lumen gentium* 8). The phrase "subsists in" replaces an earlier "is."

Although there is an ongoing debate about the precise significance of the change, the present formulation at the very least backs away from simply identifying the Church of Christ with Roman Catholicism. This, given the history of the previous four centuries, was a remarkable development. The tendency among Catholics since the Reformation to think of themselves as the one true Church and to deny any ecclesial significance to Protestant communities is well known. Individual members of those communities may well have been seen as living in the grace of Christ, but this was understood to be the case not because but in spite of the Churches to which they belonged. The shift that the present text represents was one of the first fruits of the ecumenical sensitivity that was so distinctive a feature of the whole council.

Mention has already been made of the all but revolutionary character of Vatican II in regard to the Catholic Church's attitude to ecumenism. The modern ecumenical movement began in the early years of the present century. It grew out of the experience of people in the foreign missions. The scandal of disunity among the missionaries was manifest. The impetus came from Anglicans and a cross section of Protestants and soon took a two-pronged approach issuing in what came to be known as Faith and Order, and Life and Works. The former dealt with questions of doctrine and ministry, while the second sought practical collaboration at the level of social witness. The two movements were eventually brought together in the founding in 1948 of the World Council of Churches. By this time a number of Orthodox Churches were actively involved in the process. At different stages in the history of the movement invitations were extended to the Catholic Church to take part. The official response was always negative. It seems to have been motivated by a fear of "false eirenicism," a fear that people might be satisfied with a lowest common denominator resulting in the loss of elements of the gospel truth.

Vatican II represented the reversal of this attitude. Recognizing the ecumenical movement as inspired by the Spirit, the Catholic Church now solemnly committed itself to it. In a special document it spelled out what it called "principles for Catholic ecumenism." Perhaps the most simple and yet far-reaching of these was the advice to Catholics that in approaching other Christians they should focus on what unites rather than on what divides. The document itself began the process by calling attention to fundamental agreements in regard to faith and practice. It recognized the presence of grace and the Spirit in the lives of all believers and praised in particular the Protestant reverence for the Scriptures. It went beyond traditional approaches to the eucharist, which focused almost exclusively on validity, to stress the obvious religious reality that all Christians in their differenct ways celebrate in it. Distinguishing among the Orthodox, Anglican and Protestant traditions it called attention to the fact that parallels with Catholicism are more or less marked in them. Although particular emphasis was given to the ecclesial reality of the Orthodox Churches, those communities that issued from the Reformation were also recognized in a theologically significant way as being Churches or ecclesial communities. It was this recognition more than anything else that led to the affirmation that the Church of Christ "is" not, but rather "subsists in" the Roman Catholic Church.

The council began a process in this area the end result of which is far from clear. The most immediate effect was the creation of a more open and positive atmosphere. Dialogues and conversations of an official and unofficial nature were put into place. In North America a considerable effort was made to set up inter-denominational working groups to foster common witness in regard to social and cultural issues. In some cases theological education, including the preparation of future clergy, began to be carried out in an ecumenical environment.

All these activities which were called for by Vatican II but which by now have gone well beyond the letter of the council's documents, have deepened the appreciation of many Catholics of the profoundly Christian and ecclesial nature of the other traditions. No matter how strongly one maintains the conviction that the Church of Christ continued in an unbroken way in the Catholic tradition, it is clear that the great divisions between East and West and later within the West tore at and weakened that unity at the most profound level. Fundamental Christian insights and sensitivities were lost, and this loss had repercussions for the way that the gospel was experienced within Catholicism.

Many examples could be given to illuminate what is meant. In regard to ecclesiology itself, the division between the East and the West was a major factor in the one-sidedly juridical way in which the Western tradition approached almost all questions related to the Church. The focus tended to be on power and authority, validity and jurisdiction. The dominant model became progressively more institutional and legal. In the East, ecclesiology was more sacramental and more concerned with the Holy Spirit. The attempt to reintegrate some of these values into Western ecclesiology was one of Vatican II's most significant contributions.

Something analogous can be said of the split in the Western Church at the time of the Reformation. The Protestant insistence on Scripture and on preaching was counteracted by a renewed Catholic emphasis on the sacraments. There even developed a kind of caricature that saw the one as the Church of the word and the other as the Church of the sacraments. Such a division impoverishes everyone. From the beginning and then in a developed way in the patristic period, Christianity was deeply conscious of being a religion of word and sacrament. The task of the bishop, Augustine once said, is to break the bread of the word and the bread of the eucharist.

The bilateral dialogues that were instituted after the council between the Roman Catholic and other Churches have produced agreed statements on various aspects of faith. Some of these, such as the Final Report of the Anglican—Roman Catholic International Commission on ministry, eucharist and authority, raise important questions for the Catholic Church's self-understanding. If recognition is given to these statements as authentic formulations of faith, then practical steps will have to follow in terms of a mutual recognition of orders and of intercommunion. The goal of some form of visible unity seems more possible now than at the time of the council.

Ecumenical developments have forced Catholic theologians to rethink their understanding of Church unity. Vatican II began the process by insisting that unity is not to be conceived as uniformity. It went so far as to say that it is an ecumenical responsibility to "preserve a proper freedom in the various forms of spiritual life and discipline, in the variety of liturgical rites, and even in the theological elaborations of revealed truth"(Decree on Ecumenism 4). It reiterated this point in regard to the Orthodox Churches the authority and antiquity of whose distinctive traditions it celebrated as enriching the total Christian heritage.

The model of sister Churches with distinctive spiritual, liturgical, canonical and theological traditions is something that the Roman Church has been quick to adopt in regard to Eastern Christianity. Paul VI used the same language in speaking of the Churches of the Anglican Communion. In both cases it is obvious that the ideal of unity that is operative admits of considerable diversity. Although this ideal is sometimes described as organic unity, the goal of ecumenical efforts is clearly not some kind of superchurch. Most ecumenists think of it as a communion of Churches analogous to the situation in antiquity with its loose though real unity among the patriarchal sees.

At regular intervals during the post-conciliar period people have lamented the weakening or the demise of the ecumenical spirit. That much of the enthusiasm of the late 60's has died down and that individual Church leaders tend to act in ways that are shockingly unecumenical cannot undermine the work that has been done nor can it lessen the nature of the ecumenical imperative that Vatican II recognized to be part of the Church's contemporary mission. Both success and failure underline the eschatological nature of perfect unity. The whole Church, Catholic and Orthodox, Anglican and Protestant, is a pilgrim Church, still very much on the way. The fact that visible unity remains a distant goal should not depress Christians but rather spur them on to bring it nearer.

Vatican II's commitment to ecumenism has implications for ecclesiology. The most obvious of these is the need to continue to refine the understanding of the relationship between the Catholic Church, the other Churches, and the Church of Christ. A definitive shift in this area has taken place; what is required is further theological clarification. Closely related to this development is the manner in which the ideal of unity has to be reconceived. A different kind of implication, but equally important, is the awareness that ecumenism and ecumenical sensitivity are parts of the contemporary mission of the Church. The pursuit of Christian unity has been recognized as flowing from the express will of Christ and as being inspired by his Spirit. The unity that already exists is something to celebrate; it also impels us to approach all other aspects of the Church's life and mission in ways that reinforce and do not undermine it.

Talk of "ecumenism" at the council, as in the world in general at that time, almost invariably was restricted to the pursuit of Christian unity. Since then the word has come to be applied on a much wider basis. John Paul II followed this practice in his first encyclical by concluding his reflections on ecumenism with a general statement about non-Christian religions. Here, too, he said, efforts have to be made to draw close together. This will be achieved "through dialogue, contacts, prayer in common (and) investigation of the treasures of human spirituality" (*Redemptor hominis* 6).

In the past the relation of the Church to those outside itself was primarily seen in terms of mission. Entrusted with the gospel of Christ, the Church's task was to go forth and to make disciples of all nations (cf Mt 28:19f). More often than not other religions were lumped together as manifestations of paganism, having little or no positive religious value. Unfortunately this attitude, for all the laudable intent to preach Christ, was often accompanied by manifestations of cultural imperialism. The failure of Church authorities to learn from the so-called Chinese rites controversy reinforced a tendency to identify Christianity with its European forms.

Vatican II's insistence on the importance of respect for, and dialogue with, other religions came as a surprise to most Catholics. It probably also appeared to many to be of peripheral interest. The recent dramatic increase, however, in the presence of representatives of these traditions in many parts of European and North American society brings the issue closer to home. Here as elsewhere the Church itself stands to learn from such a dialogue. Other peoples and cultures have developed or maintained values and sensitivities that are not a part of the modern Western heritage. These include religious values that could be beneficially integrated into Christian understandings of creation and of grace. Openness in this area raises questions about the role of Christ and therefore of his Church in relation to universal salvation. That Catholicism is positive about the presence of grace to all people is a given. In regard to what it implies for a theological understanding of the other religions, there is as yet no real consensus.

Vatican II's document on non-Christian religions was developed as a response to a desire of John XXIII and of many bishops that something be said about the Church's attitude to Judaism. This is an important topic with more historical and theological ramifications than can be dealt with here. In the context of an outline of some of the issues involved in a contemporary ecclesiology, two major points might be made. The first of these has to do with anti-semitism and the second with a renewed understanding of the relation in God's plan of salvation between Church and Synagogue.

Although the Vatican II document nowhere explicitly mentions the Holocaust, the mass murder of six million European Jews at the hands of the Nazis during World War II was very much in the minds of those who insisted on the need for a statement. The Holocaust raises profound moral and religious questions for all of Western society. Although part of a larger pattern of war and genocide, it was in many ways unique. In an extraordinarily systematic and inhuman fashion, men, women, and children throughout Europe were brutally seized and transported to death camps for no other reason than that they were Jews.

Since the council there has been a growing awareness among scholars that the perverse racial theories propagated by the Nazis and others were built up on, and to some degree were nourished by, a centuries-old tradition of Christian anti-semitism. Although relatively few contemporary Church people are aware of this history, it is a real one and helps to explain why this kind of racism is woven so deeply into the fabric of Western society.

An ecclesiology worthy of its subject must include a self-critical component. The Church is in many ways a sinful Church. It is far from embodying all that is implied in such images as the body of Christ and the temple of the Spirit. The NT ideal of the pure and spotless bride of Christ will only become a reality at the end of time. And so it is that themes like conversion and renewal have a place at the heart of ecclesiology. These, of course, presuppose self-knowledge. Before one can be moved to conversion one must recognize one's sin. The story of Nathan's confrontation with David offers a paradigm. It is only the prophetic word that allows the king to realize the implications of his relationship to Bathsheba (2 Sam 12:1-15).

There are similarities between the situation of an individual like David and a community like the Church. Loyalty to authority and tradition can blind otherwise intelligent and sensitive people to what is destructive and scandalous in its behavior. Here prophets are necessary, people who truly see what is going on and who have the courage to say it. Now, as in biblical times, such people are rarely appreciated, at least not while they are alive.

That some believers have learned from the history of Christian anti-semitism and felt the call to conversion, is a sign of hope. It is an experience that needs to be shared more widely. An analogous kind of self-criticism is required in other areas including Third World poverty, the missionary attitude to non-European cultures, and the role of women in Church and society. For the well-being of the Church a contemporary ecclesiology must foster and encourage critical and prophetic voices within it.

Medieval art often portrayed the Church and the Synagogue as two women, one free and triumphant and the other bound and blindfolded. Traditional theology assumed that the Church was the exclusive heir of all the hopes and covenants of Israel. Judaism, it was thought, had ceased to exist in any religiously significant way after the coming of Jesus. Here was a teaching that helped to feed traditional anti-Jewish sentiment among believers. The renewed dialogue has brought home to many Christians how simplistic and unfair such a view is. The extraordinary survival of Judaism for so long and in the face of such overwhelming odds attests to its religious vitality and demands that Christians think again about its continuing significance as an instrument of salvation. Here is something that touches the very heart of the Church's self-understanding. The new emphases at the council call for further theological development. It will take the form of a nuanced understanding of the relationship between the first and the second covenants and of the relation of both to the fact that Christians and Jews remain pilgrim peoples still moving towards that end time in which alone perfection is to be achieved.

Some of the most difficult issues facing the contemporary Church have to do with its mission. At times in the past the question of mission seemed to be fairly straightforward. Instituted by Christ and endowed with teachings and sacraments and a clearly defined pastoral leadership, the Church's task was to bring more and more people into its orbit and to provide them with the knowledge and grace they required in order to achieve eternal salvation. As profoundly anchored in society as the Church was through its organizations and structures, its focus was resolutely on the next life. Even moral responsibility was preached primarily in terms of its implications for eternity. Some lines of conduct led to heaven and others to hell, and that finally was the most important thing that could be said about them.

There are, of course, innumerable nuances that could be brought to this picture. Once the Church became a dominant force in political and cultural life, its leaders and religious communities were involved in all aspects of society: in education and in health care, in what today would be called social welfare and in the arts. The doctrine of creation was always there to remind people that this world came from God and that in spite of all sin it remained radically good. A positive view of the relationship between creation and redemption was a central factor in accounting for the optimism and energy that helped to create medieval Christendom. Ironically, it is more in the modern period with its growing secularization that believers became progressively more schizophrenic. Religion and Church had to do with grace and with the next life. This world was an arena for purely human endeavors.

The history of Catholic social teaching in the present century suggests a very different view. Although the focus initially with *Rerum novarum* of Leo XIII was on European society and on the phenomenon of industrialization, by the time of John XXIII it had expanded to a world-wide horizon and embraced the whole range of issues associated with justice and peace. Paul VI related these last two themes and argued that in the modern context they are inseparable. "Peace is something that is built up day after day, in the pursuit of an order intended by God, which implies a more perfect form of justice among (all people)" (*Populorum progressio* 76).

From the beginning of his pontificate John Paul II has repeatedly referred to Vatican II and its ecclesiology. He has insisted on the fundamental importance of two of its documents, *Lumen gentium* and *Gaudium et spes*. Together they represent the major facets of the council's vision of a renewed Church. The first deals with its inner life, and the second with the contribution that it is to make to the world at large. The latter is in fact addressed "to the whole of humanity." It proclaims that because the Church is made up of human beings all that affects human life, in no matter what way, is part of its concern. Precisely as members of the body of Christ believers are called to contribute to the building up of a more humane society.

The theological basis for this view is to be found in the unity of creation and redemption. Christ's coming was meant to overcome sin and therefore to help humankind work at making creation what God had intended it to be from the beginning. Although the gospel proclaims definitive salvation with God, it in no way intends to weaken responsibility for this world. "Christ is now at work in the hearts of [people] by the power of his Spirit; not only does he arouse in them a desire for the world to come but he quickens, purifies, and strengthens the generous aspirations of [all] to make life more humane and conquer the earth for this purpose" (*Gaudium et spes* 38). A firm hope in eschatological fulfillment should in no way undermine commitment to the present life; it should rather deepen and strengthen it. It is after all this life and our contribution to it that is meant to live in a transfigured state in the eternal kingdom.

The way in which, according to the council, the Church can best exercise its responsibility in the world is related to its vision of the human person. At the heart of contemporary social issues is the question of the dignity and the rights of human beings both as individuals and as members of various groups. Here more than anywhere else is a place where the Church as Church has some kind of expertise; it has a vision and a conviction that if communicated could make a difference.

Reiterating this view in his first encyclical, John Paul II emphasized how faith in Christ deepens one's sense of the dignity of people. Every human being "without any exception whatever—has been redeemed by Christ," and with every human being "without any exception whatever—Christ is in a way united, even when [the person] is unaware of it" (*Redemptor hominis* 14). He then went on to examine in the light of this fundamental conviction the various threats—economic, military, and social—with which people today are confronted. He ended the section by affirming his support for the United Nations and especially for its Declaration of Human Rights. In his speech at the UN in October 1979 he argued that it is the disregard of human rights that leads to war and that respect for them is absolutely essential for peace.

From the beginning Christians have known that love of God and love of neighbor are inseparable. If at times they were tempted to restrict that love to their own, the parable of the good Samaritan was there to recall that authentic Christian love admits of no exceptions. In a similar fashion the solemn last judgment scene in Matthew 25 has been a continual reminder that ultimate success or failure before God is to be measured in terms of whether and to what degree people have responded to the poor, the sick, and the needy of every kind.

The challenge for the contemporary Church is to understand what these traditional values mean within the economic and political structures of a technological and interdependent world. John Paul II has made one of his highest priorities the attempt to do just that. It is central to his encyclical on labor, *Laborem exercens*, and is a part of the message that he proclaims on all his trips. During his 1984 visit to Canada he said that love of neighbor today means "respect for persons, [for] their freedom,

[for] their dignity...; respect for human rights...; the refusal of violence and torture; concern for the less fortunate categories, for women, for laborers, for the unemployed, for immigrants; establishment of social measures for greater equality and justice, for all men and women, regardless of individual interests or privileges; the will to live a simple life and to share...; a more universal openness towards the basic needs of the less fortunate countries, in particular those that are referred to as the 'South'..."(*Canada: Celebrating Our Faith*, Boston, 1985, pp. 159f).

The pope came back to this last point in the context of a homily on Matthew's account of the last judgment. Warning his hearers that they must not be satisfied with "an 'individualistic' interpretation of Christian ethics," he said that in this passage Christ "is speaking of the whole universal dimension of injustice and evil. He is speaking of what today we are accustomed to call the North-South contrast." He went on to affirm that "in the light of Christ's words, this poor South will judge the rich North. And the poor people and poor nations... will judge those people who take their goods away from them, amassing to themselves the imperialistic monopoly of economic and political supremacy at the expense of others" (*ibid* pp. 272f).

In passages like these the old and the new come together. The passion and concern are the passion and concern of the prophets and of Jesus. The specific references attempt to relate their teaching to contemporary conditions. It is the same process that is at the heart of what is called liberation theology. Developed primarily in Latin America as a means for translating the vision of *Gaudium et spes* into the local political and economic situation, it begins with the experience of the oppressed. The Church for liberation theology is not simply a community that is to be concerned for the poor, it is made up in a privileged way of the poor. The theme of Church and poverty was raised at Vatican II. The NT affirmation that a sign of the messianic era was the fact that the poor had the gospel preached to them, led to the insight that God cares in a special way for the poor and that he calls his Church to do the same. In the famous base communities of Latin America small groups of believers gather together and reflect on their experience in the light of the gospel. The hope is that it will provide the insight and the courage to move them to action. Within this context the notion of the preferential option for the poor takes on special meaning. Here society is analyzed and the gospel is read from the perspective of those who are at the bottom.

In parts of Europe the same concerns have given birth to what is known as political theology. Here, once again, the desire is that the Church will learn to speak concretely to the contemporary world and thus make its critical and positive contribution to the overcoming of humanity's ills. A major concern of political as well as liberation theology is to show how the mission of the Church necessarily includes a social dimension. Christian salvation has implications in the present as well as in the future. This conviction was given an authoritative expression by the 1971 synod of bishops. "Action on behalf of justice and participation in the transformation of the world fully appear to us as a constitutive dimension of the preaching of the Gospel, or, in other words, of the Church's mission for the redemption of the human race and its liberation from every oppressive situation" (*Renewing the Earth*, ed. by D. O'Brien and T. Shannon, Garden City, 1977, p. 391).

Some of the ways that Church leaders have attempted to respond to the challenge contained in this statement reflect the interrelatedness of recent developments in ecclesiology. In the earlier part of the century Catholic social teaching was proclaimed primarily, if not exclusively, in papal encyclicals. Now it is finding a variety of instruments and is being developed at the local as well as the international level. Concrete situations vary from country to country and from continent to continent. If what is said is to have any real impact it must be related to specific conditions. A realization of this provoked the historic meetings of the Latin American episcopate at Medellin and Puebla. It has also sparked many national hierarchies to publish documents on social and economic issues as these affect their respective countries. Here again we encounter the importance of national and regional Churches and the fruitfulness of a healthy pluralism. Paul VI explicitly recognized the need for such local adaptation in a 1971 letter marking the eightieth anniversary of *Rerum novarum*. In the face of "widely varying situations," the pope said, "it is difficult for us to utter a unified message and to put forward a solution which has universal validity." It is up to local Christian communities "to analyze with objectivity the situation which is proper to their own country" and in the light of the gospel and the general principles of Catholic social doctrine "to discern the options and commitments which are called for in order to bring about the social, political and economic changes seen in many cases to be urgently needed." In the pope's view the major responsibility here lies with the laity. They are, however, urged to collaborate with bishops, other Christians and all people of good will (*Renewing the Earth*, pp. 353f).

The method followed by the American bishops in the writing of their documents on peace and on the economy offers a paradigm for a new mode of exercising the magisterial office. Lay people, including experts in a wide range of areas, were involved at every step of the way. The fact that the documents went through drfts that were published and that people in general had a chance to respond to them broadened the participation dramatically. It is in procedures like these that Vatican II's call for the full and active participation of everyone in the life and mission of the Church takes on concrete meaning. The whole process was clearly an exercise in co-responsibility.

One of the specific themes addressed in the council's treatment of the relation of the Church to the contemporary world was that of culture. It is a theme that has become more central in recent years. In 1982 John Paul II instituted a pontifical council for culture. Its task is to facilitate dialogue between the Church and contemporary cultures and to be an instrument by which the Church might be of assistance to particular cultures in their efforts to survive and flourish. In 1980 in Paris the pope addressed the issue of culture in an important speech before UNESCO. It is a theme to which he has returned repeatedly on his trips where he has shown himself especially sensitive to the problems of ancient and native cultures threatened by the rapid spread of a one-sidedly technological and scientific mentality.

The theme of Church and culture has been present throughout this book. One of the values of the image of the people of God is that it allows us to think of the Church not statically but dynamically, not abstractly but concretely. It is neither a walled garden nor a fortress set upon a hill.Even the image of the boat riding upon the waves is inadequate to suggest how profoundly it is immersed in history. The Church is a human phenomenon, a movement, a people on the march. It lives in history and in a variety of cultures. As these are born and flourish, wither and die, so the Church enters into and shares their destiny without every totally identifying with any one of them. Part of being a universal Church is to be to some degree transcultural; part of being an eschatological community is to be deeply aware of the limits of every culture.

Paul VI in his 1975 Apostolic Exhortation on Evangelization in the Modern World reaffirmed the importance of a missionary activity that reaches to the very depths of human culture. If the fundamental mission of the Church is to keep alive and proclaim the gospel message of the kingdom, it will only do this to the degree that it succeeds in evangelizing "culture and cultures (not in a purely decorative way, as it were, by applying a thin veneer, but in a vital way, in depth and right to their very roots)" (20). It was the Church's attempt to do this in the past that constitutes one of the great dramas of its history.

Like all human communities the Church was born at a particular time and in a particular culture; from the beginning its language and structures, its mentality and practices were influenced by that fact. Early Christianity was largely a Jewish phenomenon. Jesus was a Jew, as were all his first disciples. In the post-resurrection period a distinction was soon made between Jewish Christians of Aramaic and those of Greek background. Their different heritages help to explain the pluralism of the NT. Before long one of the most difficult and challenging changes in the history of Christianity was underway, the change from a fundamentally Jewish-Christian Church to one that would be at home in the Hellenistic culture of Greco-Roman society. The cultural distance from Jerusalem to Athens was experienced by some as an unbridgeable gulf.

What is most distinctive about Catholic Christianity came to the fore in this early and in some sense paradigmatic process of cultural adaptation. There was a concern for both continuity and *aggiornamento*. If it was clear that the gospel and the apostolic tradition had to be defended at all costs, it was equally clear that the very nature of the Church's mission demanded creativity and openness in developing ways of preaching the mystery of Christ to peoples and cultures whose backgrounds did not include the experiences and hopes of Israel. And so the God of Abraham was related to the God of the philosophers and Christ was proclaimed as the logos whose mysterious presence could already be discerned in what was best in the cultures of Greece and of Rome.

Some Christians have judged that the Church went too far in the process of Hellenization. Most, however, would admit that it was only by doing what it did that it was able to be more than a tiny sect condemned to live on the edge of the dominant culture of the time.

Echoing Paul VI, John Paul II has repeatedly decried as one of the great tragedies of our time the divorce between faith and culture. Almost everywhere in the Western world the older synthesis has collapsed. A new culture has arisen, one that is marked by science and technology and by what the pope calls "consumerism," one that when it admits of religious and moral values at all is radically pluralistic. The challenge today for the Church is to find ways of being present in this culture that will not corrupt and undermine its identity but will permit it to fulfill its mission of "bringing the Good News into all the strata of humanity, and through its influence transforming humanity from within and making it new"(*Evangelization in the Modern World* 18).

Culture figures in the Church's mission in another way. According to John Paul II's analysis culture is a profoundly human reality the roots of which lie ultimately in the minds and hearts, the thoughts and aspirations, of the men and women who create and sustain it. An attitude of fundamental respect for culture flows, therefore, from a sense of human dignity and is inseparable from respect for people. This is why the fostering and defending of cultures, especially those which are weak or vulnerable to attack is part of the Church's mission.

The relationship between Church and culture is not only complex, it is also constantly undergoing change. If the Church contributes to culture, it also benefits from it. This, according to the council, has been the case from the beginning. Different cultures have provided the Church with a variety of insights in its ongoing effort to plumb the mystery of human life. They have also challenged and stimulated it to articulate its faith in new and different ways. The effort to do this "must ever be the law of all evangelization. In this way it is possible to create in every country the possibility of expressing the message of Christ in suitable terms and to foster vital contact and exchange between the

Church and different cultures" (*Gaudium et spes* 44). The challenge in this regard presented by the contemporary situation has not yet been fully met.

The historical relationship between the Church and culture has varied. In some cases Christians have been critical in regard to culture or at least to a particular culture; at other times they have made it an important element in their own self-definition. It is clear that an adequate view will have to include both elements; it is equally obvious that what might be required at one moment, could be hopelessly inadequate at another. The example of Nazi Germany with the more or less disastrous responses of the Churches to it remains as a salutary warning.

The whole Church, both lay and ordained, shares in the prophetic vocation of Christ. It must always be alert to what is negative and destructive in a culture and have the courage to criticize it clearly and forcefully. As a community rooted in the mystery of the incarnation and convinced of the positive relation between creation and redemption, however, its relation to culture can never be simply negative. It is called to foster what is positive in particular cultures so that they will be vehicles for furthering authentic values. While respecting the autonomy of secular structures, believers must attempt in a very real sense to Christianize them. John Paul II formulated the ideal in a particularly striking way when he spoke of "Christ animating the very center of all culture" (*Canada* p. 221).

The Church: An Introductory Bibliography

Abbott, W. ed., *The Documents of Vatican II,* New York: Guild Press, 1966

Butler, C., *The Theology of Vatican II,* Westminster, Md.: Christian Classics, 1981

Chittister, J., *Women, Ministry and the Church,* New York: Paulist, 1983

Dulles, A., *Models of the Church,* Garden City, N.Y.: Doubleday, 1974

_____, *The Resilient Church,* Garden City, N.Y.: Doubleday, 1977

_____, *A Church to Believe In,* New York: Crossroad, 1982

Flannery, A. ed., *Vatican Council II: the Conciliar and Post Conciliar Documents,* Collegeville: The Liturgical Press, 1975

Granfield, P., *The Papacy in Transition,* Garden City, N.Y.: Doubleday 1980

Gremillion, J. ed., *The Church and Culture Since Vatican II: The Experience of North and Latin America,* Notre Dame; Un. of Notre Dame Press, 1985

Hebblethwaite, P., *John XXIII: Pope of the Council,* London: Geoffrey Chapman, 1984

Lohfink, G., *Jesus and Community: The Social Dimension of Christian Faith,* New York: Paulist; Philadelphia: Fortress, 1984

Meyer, H. and L. Vischer, eds., *Growth in Agreement: Reports and Agreed Statements of Ecumenical Conversations on a World Level,* New York: Paulist; Geneva: World Council of Churches, 1984

Miller, J.M., *What Are They Saying About Papal Primacy?,* New York: Paulist Press, 1983

O'Brien, D. and T. Shannon eds., *Renewing the Earth: Catholic Documents on Peace, Justice and Liberation,* Garden City, N.Y.: Doubleday, 1977

Pawlikowski, J., *What Are They Saying About Christian-Jewish Relations?,* New York: Paulist Press, 1980

Power, D., *Gifts That Differ: Lay Ministries Established and Unestablished,* New York: Pueblo, 1980

Rahner, K., *The Shape of the Church to Come,* New York: Seabury, 1974

Segundo, J., *The Community Called Church,* Maryknoll, N.Y.: Orbis, 1973

Tillard, J.-M., *The Bishop of Rome,* Wilmington, Del.: M. Glazier, 1984